ILLNESS

OR

DISTRESS?

ALTERNATIVE MODELS
OF MENTAL HEALTH

BY

JAYANTHI BELIAPPA

CONFEDERATION OF INDIAN ORGANISATIONS (UK)

Produced by Roger Booth Associates, Newcastle upon Tyne

© Confederation of Indian Organisations (UK), January 1991

ISBN: 0 9511412 3 6

CONTENTS

i

Tables

Appendices

Acknowledgements

We would like to take this opportunity to thank all the individuals and agencies who contributed to the development and completion of this project.

We are grateful to Haringey Social Services for permitting us to locate the project in the borough. Cooperation from the Asian voluntary sector within Haringey enabled us to obtain an initial idea of the community.

We have received invaluable support from the members of the Working Party through the different stages of the project. Critical appraisal from them proved constructive in reducing deficiencies in the argument. Whatever faults remain are entirely our own.

We wish to thank our interviewers who had to cope with many disappointments. The most valuable input into the project has been the experiences rendered by the informants themselves. We are indebted to them for their time and their patience.

My very special thanks to my colleagues at the Confederation of Indian Organisations (UK). I have been fortunate to have the support of Tanzeem Ahmed whose analytical skills and sensitivity to the subject of the research helped to clarify many issues. Bhanu Nagda has been a source of great support with the administrative aspect of the research.

Forward

This report examines many of the major concerns facing the Asian community. The study specifically addresses the issue of mental health. It proposes the validity of alternative models of mental health and the need to incorporate the user's "frame of reference" into the agenda of planning and delivery of mental health care services. It is unfortunate that a scarce amount of literature exists on the subject. This report will hopefully awaken those who are concerned to investigate further the mental health needs of ethnic minorities, to formulate theoretical models which are more appropriate to these communities and at the same time use this information to bring about action that will actually assist those in need.

The research is placed within the broader context of advocating for equal opportunities which has been the foremost concern of the Confederation of Indian Organisations (U.K.). There is at present a lack of government commitment to meeting the needs of ethnic minorities. This has been reflected in the White paper on community care, in which the needs of ethnic minorities are marginalised. There is a real danger that unless the mental health needs of the Asian community are put on the political agenda and more resources are allocated to meeting these needs at an early stage, a significant section of those who are most vulnerable within ethnic minority communities will face chronic physical and mental health problems which can not be catered within the system of care that exists at present. It is only through concerted action that many of the problems which Asians and other immigrants face, will be resolved.

Kanti Nagda
Secretary General
Confederation of Indian Organisations

Preface

This is an ambitious study. It is a bold attempt to explore some of the major factors which influence the delivery of mental health services to the Asian community.

Survey after survey confirms that discrimination faced by immigrants is widespread in terms of housing, employment, education, criminal justice system and in health. There have been many initiatives, such as the Community Relations Act 1976 and various equal opportunity strategies to promote equality in the community and partnership in the workplace. The express purpose of these has been to improve the quality of life for immigrants, however, these have been patchy and ad hoc.

A number of studies have been carried out in recent times on immigrants, and in particular Asians who may have language difficulties. The information suggests that more Asians are admitted to psychiatric institutions than their indigenous counterparts, often by-passing general practitioners, community psychiatric nurses, social workers and other helping agencies. In essence, there is an alarming rate of admission to psychiatric institutions of black and ethnic minority groups (including Asians) being detained under Section 138 of the Mental Health Act 1983.

The author in her report has explored settlement patterns and the conditions of inner city deprivation which are contributing factors which face Asians accessing health services. A careful exploration of coping models using the care study provides a framework for understanding how some Asians cope with Mental Health stress.

There is a prevailing view nurtured by some professionals that Asian family ties and religious customs create solid bonds which are difficult to penetrate. This study did not address this issue.

This illuminative study has been completed at an opportune time. The White Paper 'Caring for People – Community Care in the Next Decade and Beyond', and the relevant sections of the National Health Service and Community Care Act 1990, proposed profound changes in philosophy and procedures in community care services for adult users, both for statutory authorities and mixed economy.

Since the proposals are a challenge for professional practitioners, amongst whom some are Social Services Department workers and those in the voluntary and private sector, this Report's findings and recommendations should provide valuable information of the needs of Asians, which could be taken forward by the Local Authority, District Health Authority and Family Health Services Authority into the planning of the Community Care Plans.

Henderson Holmes
Assistant Director
Haringey Social Services

Members of the Working Party

Tanzeem Ahmed.	Director Confederation of Indian Organisations (U.K.)
Veena Bahl.	Departmental Adviser, Ethnic Minority Health, Department of Health
Ian Bassham.	Development Planning Officer Social Services, Haringey Council
Naomi Connelly.	Research & Social Policy Officer Greater London Citizens Advice Bureau
Dr. Suman Fernando.	Consultant Psychiatrist Chase Farm Hospital, Enfield
Tessa Harding.	Consultant – Management & Staff Development – National Institute of Social Work
Henderson Holmes.	Assistant Director Social Services, Haringey
Brigid MacCarthy.	Academic Unit St. Bernard's Wing Ealing Hospital
Dr. Parimala Moodley.	Consultant Psychiatrist Maudsley Hospital
Rafat Mughal.	Development Worker South East Mind
Kanti Nagda.	Secretary General, Confederation of Indian Organisations (UK)

Introduction

This report addresses some of the issues concerning the mental health of the Asian community in Britain.* In recent years an abnormally high admission rate of ethnic minority groups into psychiatric hospitals has been reported. It is suggested that higher rates of psychological disorders are prevalent among groups from Africa, the Old Commonwealth, India and Pakistan whereas those from Cyprus, Malta and native Britons had the lowest rates. Asians fall into the first category and it is relevant to ask what it is that makes them more vulnerable.

Knowledge of mental health problems amongst immigrants in Britain is largely based on data derived from those who have contacted the services, using G.P. lists and hospital admissions as the sample frame (Cochrane 1977). However, treated prevalence rates may be biased because of problems of access to clinical services and the fact that presentation of symptoms could vary greatly across cultures. Data drawn from an institutional perspective further limits insights into concealed psychological disturbances and the life contexts in which these occur.

This research uses a community perspective to explore epidemiological data based on perceptions of the general population. For this purpose data has been drawn from a random sample of 98 Asian individuals resident in Haringey.

The research aims to:

- increase knowledge and awareness of the community's "frame of reference" – this includes religious and cultural categories that affect behaviour and structure prevalent attitudes to mental health.
- explore local and historical contexts in which neurotic symptoms are most likely to be experienced and how these vary for different age and gender groups.
- gain insight into models of coping with stressful experiences and the support networks commonly used.
- assess the undetected prevalence of minor psychological disorders that could potentially lead to more severe manifestations.
- evaluate the awareness and uptake of local services.
- identify areas of need for those who are vulnerable.

Throughout this report the Asian community is not taken to comprise a homogeneous population. Variations arising from differences in language, religion, culture and historical experiences would make generalisations difficult.

1

A Note on Terminology

The report attempts to reach conceptualisations of mental health as it is defined by the community. Accordingly, classifications such as "mental-illness" and "depression" derived from the Western Medical Model are treated with caution. Emotional disturbances are traditionally described as 'sorrow', 'anxiety' or as a 'burden' and therefore are not seen as pathological within Asian cultures. The absence of an equivalent South Asian term for "depression" raises interesting questions on certain assumptions about "normality".

Differences in the way emotions are expressed and dealt with vary across cultures and are a function of the cultural shaping of normative and deviant behaviour. The "depressive syndrome" for example is a category of symptoms developed by psychiatrists to yield a homogeneous group of patients (Klienman 1977). To apply this as a universal tool would possibly lead to the danger of over-generalisation of "symptoms" that may not be relevant for cultural groups with different notions of pathological behaviour. On the other hand, symptoms that do not fit easily into these parameters could easily be missed (Fernando 1988).

As far as the Asian Communities are concerned, it is important to examine the socio-cultural context in order to explore the interpretations of mental health that are expressed and accepted. The process of migration and cultural adaption for this population could mean that categories are being re-interpreted and variations in perceptions are to be expected. From this point of view the tendency to transpose models of illness dominant in the home countries in order to explain local experience could lead to unrealistic assumptions of the immigrant population. Some of this is responsible for the static, stereotypical conceptions used to understand Asian communities.

CHAPTER 1 examines the methodology of the research. It explains the procedure used for selecting and contacting the sample, and explores the pattern of non-response. The chapter also describes the selection of interviewers and the format of the questionnaire.

CHAPTER 2 examines the relevance of placing mental health in the context of local and historical experience and picks up some of the regularities the data throws up in relation to the settlement patterns of Asian immigrants. In the sample certain specific indices of settlement have been taken into account such as life expectations, satisfaction and employment.

CHAPTER 3 describes the main concerns expressed by the sample and evaluates which of these concerns tend to be more severe. From this a link is drawn between levels of severity and the manner in which individuals are affected by those concerns. The chapter looks at the support networks commonly used by the sample for different problems and in particular the status of the family as a support unit in the Asian community today. The models used by the sample to cope with stress are then set out, leading to a discussion of how coping models affect world view.

CHAPTER 4 takes up gender and age differentiation in the discussion of issues around employment status, settlement patterns and major concerns. The variations in male and female roles and expectations are then taken up in order to throw light on role satisfaction and the distinct spheres within which roles are seen as meaningful for males and females.

CHAPTER 5 explores whether Asians make use of conventional pathways to care especially with reference to mental health. It also raises questions on how 'normality' and 'pathology' are conceptualised in different cultures. The chapter gives an account of the general causes of ill-health, and the more specific link between stress and poor physical health. In order to facilitate this analysis, stress is linked to concerns and life events. The chapter leads to a discussion of reasons for which G.Ps are seen, experiences with G.Ps as reported by the sample and the kind of problems that are taken to the G.P.

CHAPTER 6 attempts to reach an understanding of the informant's own frame of reference in the definition of mental health. Some of the general relationships between life experiences, roles and distress are at first examined. Positive and negative coping mechanisms used by the segment of the sample experiencing distress leads to a discussion on the needs of those vulnerable. Certain illustrative cases are drawn to describe the specific links these individuals, who see themselves as emotionally distressed, are making in defining their own mental health.

CHAPTER 7 evaluates the uptake of services by the sample of the Asian community. The chapter looks at awareness of services, whether information reaches out to the community, and which of the services are used. The barriers experienced in the use of services are described. The sample's views are then recorded on services lacking for the Asian community in Haringey.

CHAPTER 1

Methodology

The Population

There has been a tendency for particular minority groups to congregate in certain localities and Haringey is no exception in this respect. The main ethnic groups in Haringey are Afro-Caribbeans, Asians and Greek/Turkish Cypriots. Haringey has one of the largest proportion of ethnic groups in the UK.

The best indication of the size of Haringey's ethnic minority population is the proportion of Haringey's residents living in households of which the head of the household was born outside the UK, because most of those born in this country from this group are included in these figures (Census 1981).

Nearly half of Haringey's population live in such households compared to only a quarter in Greater London as a whole.

There is a clustering of Asians in the eastern half of the borough. The 1981 Census shows the following electoral wards to have a high proportion of Asians.

Bowes Park	5.1%
Green Lanes	4.1%
Harringay	6.5%
Hornsey Central	4.8%
Noel Park	4.9%
South Hornsey	4.1%
South Tottenham	4.1%
Tottenham Central	4.1%
Woodside	5.7%

(These figures may have changed over the past few years.)

Asians constitute 3.7 per cent of Haringey's total population. Out of these 35 per cent were born in East Africa, 47 per cent were born in India, 9 per cent were born in Bangladesh and 9 per cent were born in Pakistan (for details see Appendix 1 & 2).

The Sample

The Electoral Register has been used as the sample frame. However, using this sample frame was not without problems.

Since all the names were not listed, the sample frame only partially represented the Asian population. Sufficient time had lapsed since the register was prepared and it is likely that some people could have moved during this period.

A list of one thousand Asian names was drawn from the electoral register for wards with a relatively high proportion of Asians. Difficulties were experienced in deciphering between the surnames of Turkish Cypriots and Muslims from the subcontinent. The first name helped to make the distinction clearer. Sometimes it was possible to sort out the confusion on the basis of the way the name was spelt.

The list was then classified into language groups so that the sample would proportionately represent the various language groups in the population. Here again the naming system was used as a marker to distinguish language groups.

The sample size was targetted at 200. Using the procedure of random selection one in every five names was selected within each language group.

The unit of the sample was taken as the individual and not the household. This is important to remember because different individuals within a household could hold conflicting views.

Contacting the Sample

In the first instance a letter briefly explaining the project was posted (see Appendix 3).

Since the sample was divided into language groups each person was sent a letter in his/her language in addition to a letter in English.

This letter was followed up with a phone call by the interviewer who spoke the appropriate language. The interviewer at first introduced the project and then attempted to arrange a convenient time for the interview. Every effort was made to interview the informant on his/her own. This first contact was also used to reassure the informant that the interview would be treated with the strictest of confidence.

One of the major problems in making the first personal contact proved to be the large proportion of the sample who either did not have telephones or possessed an ex-directory number.

In these cases the first recall letter was posted (see Appendix 4). This letter carried the name of the interviewer, and their address and telephone number.

Having arranged a time either through the phone or where this was absent using the first recall letter, the interviewer made the first visit to the informant's home.

If the first visit was not successful another attempt was made to contact the informant by phone and where this was not possible a second recall letter was sent (see Appendix 5).

This was followed by the second visit. If the informant could not be contacted at the time of the second visit that name was substituted by another name which was selected using the same sampling procedure as for the original sample.

Substitution

The sampling frame included units that field investigation proved did not exist. Twenty-seven of the sample of 200 could not be accessed because they had changed addresses and their new addresses were not available. This number was subtracted from the sample size before calculating the rate of non-response. Every effort was made to substitute that portion of the sample which could not be accessed. However, restraints of time and resources prevented contact from being made with the substituted units. The size of the sample was calculated by subtracting this number (27) and the number of non-respondents (75) from the original sample. This left a final sample size of 98.

Non-Response

The rate of non-response was recorded at 43 per cent taken as an average, but interesting variations existed between the different language groups. The highest rate of non-response was experienced with the Bangladeshi segment (68%). This data supports earlier research with the Bangladeshi community (McCarthy 1988). By contrast the Gujerati sample had the lowest non-response rate of 27 per cent.

Recorded below are some of the major reasons for non-response.

1. No phone. Visited the address. Posted the second recall letter
   and called on one further occasion. No one answered the door   27

2. Responded to the phone call. Agreed a date and time for the
   interview. Was not home at the first visit or on the second visit   8

3. No phone. The potential informant was contacted at home.
   Expressed interest but too busy to participate in the interview.
   Interviewer asked to return at another date and time
   But even the second time around the informant refused
   to participate.   12

4. No phone. Answered the door but did not agree to an interview.   13

5. Refused at the time of the first phone call.   15

   Total number of non-responses   75

The reasons for non-response listed above indicate some of the common problems of contacting and arranging interviews shared by social research in general.

However, a significant number of the refusals relate to the sensitive nature of research on mental health. Two of the informants who did participate in the interview refused to have their names recorded. Many others expressed concern about issues relating to confidentiality.

At all times it was necessary first to establish rapport followed by the assurance that the information would be treated confidentially.

Interviewing

The interviewers were selected on the basis of language skills, background of community work, experience of previous interviewing and understanding of issues relating to Mental Health.

Six interviewers were selected and trained over two days on various aspects of the project, the methodology and the procedure for interviewing.

The Questionnaire

Interviews were carried out using the instrument of semi-structured question-naires. The questionnaire was designed following a pilot study based in Haringey. This study enabled us to focus on some of the issues concerning mental health.

7

The coding frame of the questionnaire was set up at the time the questionnaire was designed. It was decided to leave a number of questions open-ended in order that the responses were not predetermined. Such questions were post-coded.

The questionnaire was administered in the language of the informant and carried a set of questions that were specific to those who were either born in this country or immigrated before the age of 16.

CHAPTER 2

Local and Historical Background

The relevance of placing mental health in the context of the immigrant's local and historical experiences has been recognised (Murphy 1977), but there is little information yet available on such aspects as expectations, life satisfaction and nature of concerns to facilitate a systematic enquiry into the kind of effects such experiences could have on mental health.

"The experience and perception of mental illness are however invariably bound up with cultural and political assumptions and at the same time poverty, disadvantage, cultural change and the conflict between generations take their toll on an individual's mental health" (Littlewood and Lipsedge 1982).

In this chapter we raise some of these issues using the data collected from a sample of Asian immigrants in Haringey. It is important to bear in mind that historical experiences mean that generalisations must be treated with caution. However, it may be valuable to record some of the regularities we observed with reference to the characteristics immigrants bring with them and the ways in which they respond to social processes.

Some General Characteristics

Ninety-five per cent of the sample immigrated into this country and only 5 per cent were born here. Our observations therefore refer mainly to an immigrant population. Variations that arise for different age and gender groups will be taken up separately in Chapter 4.

Of those who immigrated into Britain, 75 per cent were originally from India, 14 per cent from Bangladesh, 7 per cent from Pakistan and 4 per cent from other countries. Of these 42 per cent were twice migrants, migrating mainly from East Africa (33%) and Mauritius (9%). In terms of self-perception the greatest number (80%) of the responses suggest that a close identity with the Asian and subcontinental ethnic matrix is retained following migration while a smaller number, 20 per cent, see themselves as British.

As far as education was concerned, 70 per cent of the sample was educated overseas, while 30 per cent had received all or part of their education in Britain. Forty-seven per cent of the category educated overseas had no formal qualifications.

Sixty-seven per cent had received partial or total educational instruction in English. Yet, the data suggests that this was not the language in which ideas and emotions were commonly expressed. When our respondents were asked in what ways life in this country was different, with specific reference to experience with the G.P., almost 50 per cent of the responses centered around language difficulties.

A quarter of those who had negative experiences put it down to language and communication barriers.

We shall now move on from these general features to some specific indices of settlement such as expectations, satisfaction and employment.

Expectations and Settlement

We shall look at the expectations held by the migrant segment of our sample at the time of migration and the extent to which these expectations were fulfilled.

Forty-one per cent of the sample were satisfied with the conditions in this country. Nine per cent were fairly ambiguous in that they had no clear idea of what to expect. The rest came into a situation characterised, as they saw it, by a higher standard of living, more promising job prospects, better housing and educational opportunities.

A majority of respondents in this latter group had immigrated from East Africa. As twice migrants, they had possibly developed more resilience and had clearer notions of what to expect. Our data indicated that they were likely to look at migration in a tangible form, as a way of restoring what had been lost and reconstructing a new successful life. Preservation of culture was more easily achieved for this group because migration was collective. Settlement in this country took place in the midst of established networks. This form of collective migration contrasted with the pattern of immigration from the subcontinent and Mauritius, which comprised primarily individuals and nuclear families.

We are not suggesting here that all immigrants from East Africa viewed migration from a positive perspective, but from within our sample, we found that despite their share of problems, the relative cultural continuity achieved from collective migration provided a firm basis for the East African Asian community.

One of them said:

"In this country, it is up to each individual to make or unmake his life. There are better opportunities. We could think of owning our house here."

Another immigrant from Kenya believed:

"Generally it is a good life and the environment is cleaner and it is easier to move about. Financially too, there's a better future here. I've felt if one works hard the rewards are always there."

"We were the only Asians in the area, it was for me to break the ice. But once that was done people bent backwards to help us. We need to think of values that are universal and human rather than sectarian."

"It's a better life with opportunities to work and study. My training in engineering helped me to start my business and stand on my own feet."

Differences in Living Conditions

Forty-five per cent of the sample did not find this country as they had expected. Eighteen per cent of this group articulated the differences in terms of living conditions and inappropriate services.

One of the informants with special needs anticipated a situation where,

"Everyone would be helpful – but because I did not know English much the school never helped with special classes."

Another lady who cared for a deaf and dumb son felt:

"Being deaf and dumb we expected our son to be helped with education, but was told that it was too late because he was already 22 years old. That was a great disappointment. He now does piece-work in a factory stitching zips on coats. He is often deeply distressed and is exhausted with long hours of work."

A student from Bangladesh who came into this country hoping to study explained:

"I hoped to study in this country, unfortunately life was very hard and expensive, therefore I had to resort to self-employment."

Another aspiring student from India remarked that she had experienced,

"great financial difficulty and emotional starvation, and felt betrayed."

A middle aged self-employed man felt a profound change in his life,

"It was a great struggle, we stayed in one room for three years. Then we bought our own house. Life is so hard that we had to work even harder to be able to survive and pay our bills."

It would be crucial to assess the effect of differences in living conditions on the mental health of our sample of immigrants and whether greater difficulty was experienced when accompanied by cultural differences. The chapter on "Mental Distress" should highlight these issues with more clarity.

Cultural Differences

A greater proportion of the respondents who did not find this country as expected (81%) interpreted the differences in cultural terms.

Table 1. – Expectations and Differences

Base. All responses which did not find this country as expected

Total	Living Conditions	Cultural differences				
		Life Unjust	Culturally Different	Language Difference	Race	Iso-lation
44	8	12	7	5	6	6

We have already seen some of the ways in which people expressed differences in living conditions. Within the cultural impediment, a third found people and life to be unpleasant and unjust, while two-thirds experienced a feeling of isolation arising from cultural and language disparities and racial discrimination.

One respondent, a Muslim store keeper in British Telecom, perceived the differences in terms of a lack of honour and respect,

"We expected respect, instead we were marginalised on the basis of the colour of our skin."

A 55 year old East African Asian who was unemployed talked of people being very unjust,

"It was very different. Language and colour was against us. Finally we were helped by our own people."

We shall now relate employment status to the manner in which cultural differences at the time of migration are being perceived in order to understand how present life circumstances can influence perceptions of the past.

Table 2. – Employment Status and Cultural Differences

Base. All responses relating to cultural differences

Employment Status	Ways in which different					
	Total	Un-just	Culturally Different	Language Difficulties	Racism	Iso-lation
Unemployed	13	3	0	1	3	0
Housewife	28	4	4	1	1	4
Self-employed	23	1	2	2	0	1
Student	4	0	0	0	0	0
Employed	24	4	1	0	2	0
N/A	6	0	0	1	0	1

The above data illustrates that variations in employment status influence interpretations of migration. Experiences in the present life situation are likely to play a part in the construction of models of the past.

The unemployed section of the sample interpreted experiences relating to migration largely in terms of racism and unjust treatment. Forty-three per cent of the housewives saw the past as characterised by cultural differences that were unjust and led to isolation. Students did not see culture as an impediment. The employed were less likely to experience language difficulties or to feel isolated but 25 per cent see the system as unjust and discriminating.

Settlement Patterns

Following our investigation into expectations and satisfaction we shall now look at settlement patterns.

Table 3. – Settlement patterns

Base. All responses

Description of Settlement	Total
Difficulties in preserving language, culture, religion	31
Difficult living conditions	15
Initial difficulties overcome	15
No problems adjusting	25
Preserved culture and religion	27

Most people were concerned about the preservation of culture and saw settlement primarily as cultural adaptation. Fifty-eight of the responses (51%) pointed to the importance of preserving culture as part of the settlement experience.

Of these, 31 faced difficulties while 27 managed to preserve their culture and religion. Fifteen of the 113 responses experienced difficulties in living conditions either due to housing problems or insecurity arising from violence and racial harassment. Another 15 responses suggested that initial difficulties had been overcome, while 25 had faced no problems adjusting in the first instance.

A closer look into the description of settlement suggests that those who were able to preserve cultural bonds were better adjusted. Conversely, where cultural bonds were broken it was more likely that difficulties in adjustment would be experienced.

It was easier to adjust when the family base was already established and cultural links were maintained.

A lady who migrated with her large extended family from Uganda said this of her settlement,

> *"We are a large family, almost sixty of us. We tend to do things together. I felt no hardships at all. We are a well-adjusted and a close-knit family and so the children are culturally strong."*

Another Asian male was so proud to be Indian that he asked:

> *"Why should we learn only English when the British did not learn the native language in India? It is equally important for the mother tongue*

to be used and studied for identity to be there. My children speak Urdu and pray. I have settled without losing my identity."

A young Asian girl in her early twenties remarked:

"When we came here we settled in Loughborough, everyone set to work. We had come here out of choice and had to learn to survive without forgetting our values."

Another young Asian said her family,

"had no difficulties in adjusting. We are a very religious family and my brother who is nineteen spends each Sunday at a religious centre."

On the other hand, those who were culturally and socially isolated found settlement much harder. Some of those had no family in this country, others became isolated because they were completely involved in hard work in order to earn a livelihood and had little time for cultural or religious pursuits.

The absence of a family network was reflected in what this lady had to say:

"I had no family or friends here. It was so difficult to preserve culture as people are spread out."

This self-employed couple believed:

"We were too busy trying to cope with the move to worry about adjusting. But now we feel a sense of alienation and loss."

An Asian male in professional work remarked:

"It is indeed very hard to keep cultural ties and identity. We Asians can only survive if we challenge racism and inequality."

A lady in semi-skilled work lamented when she said:

"We did not really ever settle down. We wavered about staying here permanently as there never really were family and friends. At the same time we worked very hard to improve the quality of our life."

Employment

Forty-five per cent of Asian immigrants over the age of 16 were unemployed and this included housewives and retired people. Some of these, 26 per cent, had had a job in the past. Unemployment was up to 24 per cent less for the category of immigrants born here or arrived before the age of 16.

For the sample as a whole, 24 were in employment, 23 were self-employed. Of those in employment, 54 per cent were in manual or unskilled work, 21 per cent in semi-skilled work and 25 per cent in skilled professions. This data supports earlier research findings on the concentration of Asians in manual labour.

For the purposes of our research, perceptions on the employment situation were collated to enhance understanding of settlement patterns. Twenty per cent of the respondents related only negative experiences with reference to the employment situation in general. Thirty-two per cent gave only positive answers and the rest had both positive and negative experiences to relate.

A qualified mechanical engineer explained his situation thus:

> "Although I have a stable job, there are limited opportunities for promotion. If something came up I would apply, but feel certain to be rejected on grounds of colour."

A council employee maintained:

> "Racism prevails in all aspects: career advancement, career development and training. It is important to combine a high degree of professional commitment with the ability to challenge racism."

A post office clerk said that she,

> "left in disgust as any promotion was withheld for no obvious reason. I faced racism and discrimination right through."

A cross-section of the comments recorded above suggest that people in skilled or semi-skilled work are more likely to experience racism overtly. Our respondents saw racism as particularly antagonistic to upward mobility.

By contrast, the frame of reference used by those in manual and unskilled work featured low pay, poor working conditions and scarce job opportunities and this accounted for 34 per cent of the negative comments.

One factory worker spoke thus:

> "The foreman takes advantage of us Asians. We have to work harder and for longer hours."

Equally, some of our respondents in unskilled work were frustrated by low pay. Many were paid as little as £2 an hour for factory work.

Others stuck to manual work for a lack of other options. An Asian female graduate who migrated from India worked, *"making slippers in a factory. I couldn't manage to find another job. I do not enjoy the work but wouldn't want to change it because it is near my home and the hours suit me. I couldn't speak English and was forced to work in the factory."*

The above data illustrates that a significant proportion of those with negative experiences in employment were not able to conceptualise racism and power. Those who did look at their employment situation in these terms were more likely to be in the skilled professions. For a majority of our sample in work, however, racism worked its way indirectly through unacceptable working conditions, insecurity in jobs and little or no opportunities for change.

This group of people are less likely to challenge racism or to politicise their experiences and are possibly more vulnerable since they felt powerless with regard to changing their life situation (see Fernando 1988).

Our data shows that from amongst those who were able to make the link between racism and working conditions, 45 per cent wanted to change their situation in the near future, as opposed to only 11 per cent from the group who did not make this link.

CHAPTER 3

Major Concerns & Models Used in Coping

We shall begin this chapter with a description of major concerns outlined by our sample of informants. We will proceed to examine the degree of severity of some of these concerns. We shall then explore support networks used for different problems and the various models people use in coping with stressful situations.

Twelve per cent of the sample had no concerns at all; 32 per cent of the responses relating to concerns were to do with the upbringing, education and values being imbibed by children, 21 per cent were concerned with issues relating to health, 18 per cent had financial worries, 11 per cent had problems with employment and 5 per cent were troubled by marital conflicts.

Concerns over Children

This set of concerns related to intergenerational conflict, education, care and safety of children. One parent with teenage children said:

"The loss of our children is the price we have paid on coming here. We spent all our early years tending over them. But now they have grown apart and are often disrespectful. They question us on everything and for some of these questions we have no answers."

Other parents expressed concern over education,

"There's no future for our children without good education. At the same time they cannot lose their identity and fit into English ways totally."

"Our kids must be in a position to do better than us. But we worry whether they will because the State Education is inadequate. Children seem to be underachieving."

The effect of the environment on children was brought up by parents,

"Our children are being exposed to external factors often alien to our culture, they have to be moderated."

Financial Concerns

A retired gentleman involved in community work linked financial problems within the Gujerati community to the dowry system,

"*Poorer people have to take a second mortgage to have their daughter married.*"

Death of the earning member endangered households, especially where the wife was not working.

This widow faced severe financial problems,

"*I couldn't pay my bills, the widow's pension came after 4 months and in the meantime I had spent all our savings.*"

A factory worker worried over the mortgage he paid for his house,

"*The house may have to be sold if payments cannot be met. When my father was alive he helped a lot. My mother is 75 and looks after the children since my wife goes to work.*"

Another self-employed person referred to the crippling effect of inflation,

"*I work twelve hours a day and yet money is short.*"

Financial concerns centred around a number of issues, prominent among them are social ones such as dowry and marriage. Others seemed to make references to delays experienced in social security payments such as widow's pension but the most common financial worries related to economic factors such as inflation and high mortgage repayments.

Health Concerns

Twenty-one per cent of the sample expressed health-related concerns. Although this was more common for the fifty-plus age group, different types of health concerns were voiced by informants in various age groups.

An older woman spoke of suffering from,

"*arthritis and diabetes. My husband suffers from these ailments too. Our son and daughter-in-law have to give up work in order to take us to hospital.*"

A younger lady in her forties was very concerned about her health at one time,

"*After a long period of cough and general weakness, I was diagnosed to have tuberculosis. Connected with this there was a tumour in my neck which was subsequently removed. Hardly had I recovered before I had to undergo a hysterectomy. Hopefully it's all over now.*"

19

Many of the health concerns were with reference to another member of the family. We will enter into a more detailed discussion on health issues in Chapter 5.

Marital Conflicts

One hundred per cent of the marital problems were reported by women and, as mentioned earlier, 5 per cent of the total number of responses on major concerns were about marital tensions. The incidence of divorce was nil within our sample which meant that for these women separation was not seen as a workable option. Some had contemplated breaking away but this was deferred on consideration of their children's future.

Severity of Concerns

The following table reflects variations in the level of severity for different concerns.

Table 4. Major Concerns and the Level of Severity

Base. All responses expressing major concern

Severity	Children	Marriage	Financial	Health	Employment
Total	33	5	18	22	11
Very Severe	1	1	0	0	3
Severe	3	4	3	6	1
Fairly Severe	16	0	8	14	4
Not Severe	13	0	7	2	3

The data brings out a correlation between certain types of concerns and the level of severity. Twelve per cent of the responses relating to children were of a very severe or severe nature. However, a majority of children's problems were seen as fairly severe or not severe. Ninety per cent of marriage-related concerns were considered severe and 10 per cent very severe. As noted earlier, the women in our sample with these concerns did not see divorce as a workable option although some had considered it. As a result, these women are locked into situations of conflict which makes them potentially vulnerable to mental distress (See Chapter 6).

Only a sixth of the financial concerns were severe and 44 per cent fairly severe. Twenty-seven per cent of health concerns were severe and 63 per cent fairly severe. Again, 36 per cent of employment-related concerns were considered very severe or severe.

Although the specifications of each of these stressful situations could vary, making generalisation unrealistic, it is tenable to suggest from the above data that those experiencing employment and marital concerns had the most severe problems.

Major Concerns and Effects

81 out of the 98 informants who constituted our sample appeared to have been experiencing major concerns. For 38 of these, the concerns had no effect; 6 were positively affected and 37 experienced a negative effect. Of the 37 who experienced a negative effect, 70 per cent saw this as manifested in the form of emotional disturbances and a third were able to link this with problems of physical health.

Some of the informants who were able to relate stressful experience to emotional states described the connection in these ways.

A young Asian housewife spoke of her deep frustration of living within domestic confines subjected to pressures from dominating in-laws.

A recently widowed lady said:

> *"I was so worried about running out of money and the loneliness of losing my husband that I couldn't eat or sleep and began to lose weight gradually."*

An Asian male who faced domestic tension was affected emotionally,

> *"My wife faces tremendous pressures from her family who are jealous that we are flourishing. She in turn takes it out on me and the children. But we will get away from all this by emigrating to Canada."*

A female factory worker said she felt nervous at the prospect of her husband becoming redundant,

> *"My husband will lose his job soon. We have to look after three children. I get nervous when I think of this as my own job is poorly paid."*

From this set of descriptions on how individuals saw themselves affected by concerns, we learn that a correspondence was seen between emotional effect and symptoms such as lack of concentration, sleeplessness, excessive tension and a feeling of nervousness. It is yet to be established whether these experiences are seen as pathological. These are issues that will be addressed in greater detail in Chapter 6.

Within this chapter, we shall consider the support networks available to those in need and whether certain networks were seen as more appropriate for particular problems.

Support Networks

Table 5 – Major Concerns & Support Networks

Base. All responses

Support networks	Total no.of resp.	Children	Marriage	Finance	Health	Empl.	Environ-mental
Cannot be helped	6	2	2	0	3	6	0
Self-help	19	7	1	6	2	0	0
Vol/Com group	32	16	2	8	1	1	0
G.P/H.V/ Soc.Worker	3	2	0	0	7	0	0
Family	13	4	0	1	5	0	0
Police/M.P.	2	0	0	0	0	0	2
Others	9	0	0	2	2	1	0
Not Answered	16	2	0	1	2	3	0
Total	100	33	5	18	22	11	2

In general, 6 per cent of the respondents felt they could not be helped; 19 per cent were unlikely to look outside for help and 32 per cent used outside/community organisations. Thirteen per cent said the family structure still existed as a support network, 3 per cent pointed to the services and 2 per cent would receive help from the police or M.P. if needed.

The data suggests that less people see the Asian family as a durable support structure and more would depend on themselves or turn to community/

voluntary organisations. A very small proportion see the statutory services as enabling. However, some networks are seen as more accessible than others for particular problems.

Two-fifths of the informants with marital problems felt they could not be helped. Forty per cent saw voluntary/community organisations as likely sources of help. The family network did not feature as a possible support network for marital issues. On the other hand, a quarter of those with health concerns used family support and 12 per cent of concerns with children were likely to be helped within the family. Twenty-one per cent of this category favoured helping themselves and 50 per cent would use voluntary/ community organisations for support with children's activities. Fifty per cent of those who faced employment problems said they could not be helped. A third of those with financial concerns were likely to help themselves and 44 per cent would seek help from outside sources.

The data brings to light that 40 per cent of those with marital and 55 per cent with employment problems see their situation as relatively irreversible and are not likely to consider existing support networks as appropriate to their needs. At the same time the data on the range of severity of concerns suggested that marriage and employment fall within the very severe or severe range. In other words, these are the people who are the most troubled and yet the least likely to be helped.

A train driver found it a great financial strain to maintain his family and honour mortgage payments but remarked:

"One has to help oneself and be prepared to change with time."

A mother concerned over giving her children the right upbringing felt,

"I am the only one who could have a major influence on my child's development."

A middle-aged lady who had just come out of two major surgeries revealed:

"But for my family as a whole and my husband in particular I would have gone virtually mad. They cared for me, looked after my children and saw to my diet."

Another young girl in her twenties experienced concerns over the health of her parents,

"My mother has breast cancer and my father died a few years ago after a long illness. Our family is very supportive. The outside world cannot help with individual problems."

Only 3 per cent considered the services as potential sources of help. One of these, the mother of children with an overweight problem, was told by her G.P. that this was hereditary and their diet would need to be monitored. She was trying but was unable to bring down their weight and felt:

"the social worker would be the right person to advise and support us."

Organisations were seen as vital pressure groups. One young person who was totally opposed to the government's monetary policies said:

"Privatisation is making life financially very difficult. You need to join an organisation. It would be easier then to pressurise the government to change its policy."

For another informant who was determined to fight discrimination,

"Support from the community is vital. We need collective means to fight. Through community centres and political channels we are active members of the anti-deportation campaign."

However, environmental and safety issues were more likely to be taken to the local M.P. or police, as 20 per cent of the responses indicate. A University student involved in a local campaign against a new road scheme was part of THORN, an action group supporting environmental issues. She was prepared to take this campaign to the local M.P.

Another young lady, for example, was concerned with violence and social abuse,

"The freedom to move around here has gone. Better policing would restore my confidence."

So far we have focused on potential sources of help. We shall now turn our attention to the coping mechanisms used by the sample.

Coping Models And World View

Table 6 – Coping Mechanisms

Base. All responses

Coping Mechanisms	%
Prayers	8
Self-Confidence	18
Crying	10
Support from family	5
Hard work	9
Talking/Counselling	8
Changing Structure	6
Support from services	3
Not Applicable	41

The data illustrates that more people turn towards their own resources when having to cope with difficulties – 18 per cent of the responses indicated the only way they could cope was through self-confidence, 8 per cent drew inner strength from prayers and 9 per cent saw hard work as a means of overcoming difficulties.

Only 8 per cent were willing to take their problem to others with a view to seeking advice or counselling. Crying was used as a means of relief by 10 per cent of the responses. Again, as little as 3 per cent drew support from the services.

The data draws attention to the fact that people within this sample prefer to internalise their problems. This is sufficient to suggest that our informants were less able to generalise their problems in order to access relevant advice or counselling.

A significant proportion of those who looked inwards, using prayer, self-confidence or hard work, were able to maintain a positive view on life. In general, 61 per cent were positive, 13 per cent negative and 9 per cent were neither positively nor negatively inclined with reference to their life situation. Seventeen per cent did not answer this question.

Table 7. – Future Life Situation

Base. All responses expressing major concerns

Life in 5 Yrs	Children	Marriage	Financial	Health
Total	33	5	18	22
Progress	9	1	5	8
Static	2	0	3	2
Deterioration	16	3	7	10
Don't know	6	1	3	2

Sixty per cent of those with marital problems believed their situation will deteriorate. Twenty-seven per cent of concerns over children were seen to improve in the future, while 48 per cent were seen as deteriorating. Almost a third with financial concerns said they would improve, while 38 per cent said they would deteriorate. Similarly, a majority of health concerns (45%) were seen to worsen in the near future.

Thus we may conclude by saying that an individual's world view and conceptions of the future are affected by the nature of the concerns and the models used to cope with these concerns.

CHAPTER 4

Gender and Age Differentiation

Our data on Asian males and females suggest some interesting variations in the way in which each of these categories conceptualise historical experience and respond to social processes of which they are a part. We believe that the gender issues emerging in this chapter could offer some understanding of why women are more vulnerable to psychological disturbances. This information could be invaluable for the targeting of services to Asian males and females.

Employment Status & Gender

Our sample comprised 35 males and 63 females; 37 per cent of the men were employed and 31 per cent self-employed. Out of those men employed 54 per cent were in semi-skilled, 23 per cent in skilled and 31 per cent in unskilled work.

Our data shows that many men who had started with manual work took to self-employment in due course.

"I began work at the shop floor and was in charge of drilling. But the work was too hard so I left to start my own business."

Another man said:

"I worked in a warehouse for four and a half years but eventually I got fed up and left since money was not enough."

Others with a professional background found themselves to be stagnating in their job,

"I worked for a company for 16 years as an accountant but job opportunities were just not there and I chose to start my own firm."

Although self-employment was a favourable option for Asian males in all forms of employment, a substantial number of those self-employed in our sample had been in manual work in the past.

This option was rather more limited for women. Although 19 per cent were in self-employment, a greater number had taken to self-employment in order to assist their spouses. Where this option did not exist, they continued in manual work.

This lady, a graduate from Pakistan, explained:

"When I came into this country seventeen years ago from Pakistan, I was the young bride expected to keep house, care for my husband and children. There wasn't the chance to go into further education and training. Now the children have grown and with it financial pressures. We have to go out and work now and where else but to factories."

While both Asian men and women are disproportionately represented in manual work more women in our sample have had to continue at these levels for lack of other options. The greatest barriers were experienced by those women who entered employment late.

Unemployment

Twenty-two per cent of the males and 50 per cent of females were unemployed. Of those women unemployed a substantial number were housewives.

It may be relevant to point out here that 50 per cent of unemployed men said they were experiencing severe stress. Within the female category, 48 per cent of the unemployed expressed health-related concerns. The link between unempioyment and vulnerability to health problems in general and mental health in particular merits further examination (see Chapter 6).

Table 8. – Ages of Children and Employment Status of Females

Base. Females

Age of Children	Total	Unemp/H-wives	Self-Empl.	Empl.	Not Appl.
	63	33	12	11	7
0-1	3	2	1	0	0
2-3	4	3	1	0	0
4-6	8	4	1	3	0
7-10	12	6	4	1	1
11-14	11	4	3	4	0
15-18	12	6	3	2	1
19-21+	28	18	5	3	0

This data shows that 27 per cent of the women who are unemployed or housewives had children under the age of 6 years. A quarter of mothers with children in the same age group were self-employed and another 27 per cent were in employment.

A third of the mothers with children between 7-14 were unemployed while more than half were in self-employment.

Table 9 – Male and Female Perceptions of Migration

Base. All responses on ways in which life was different

Ways in which life was different	Total 44	Males 16	Females 28
People/life unjust	12	5	7
Cultural diff	7	0	7
Language diff	5	3	2
Racism	6	4	2
Isolation	6	0	6
Better standard of living	2	1	1
High expenses	3	1	2
Lack of jobs	5	3	2
Weather	6	2	4
Housing problems	5	3	2
Hard work	4	2	2

This data shows that it is more likely for men to conceptualise the differences experienced on migration as based on racial discrimination. Thirty-one per cent of the responses from males pointed to people and life being unjust as compared to 25 per cent of the female responses. Only 7 per cent of the female responses could relate the differences to racism, while 25 per cent of the male responses made this link. Nineteen per cent of the male responses referred to language difficulties while only 7 per cent of the female responses indicated this as a difference.

On the other hand, 25 per cent of the female responses described migration as causing cultural deprivation, while none of the male responses touched on this aspect of migration.

It is plausible to suggest from the above data that within our sample Asian men are possibly more affected by problems of race and power leading to inequality while females were initially affected by the chasm between the two cultures leading to isolation.

Employment Status and Description of Settlement

We examined whether employment influenced the way women perceived settlement patterns. Nine per cent of the employed women interpreted settlement in terms of cultural differences as opposed to 31 per cent in the unemployed category. Forty-five per cent of the women in employment said they had no difficulties in adjusting and did not face isolation.

Fourteen per cent of the women who were unemployed experienced inter-generational problems in bringing up children in comparison to 9 per cent in the employed group.

The above data highlights the fact that women in employment are more able to rationalise cultural differences and are likely to develop positive attitudes towards cultural preservation. They appear better able to use a selective approach and encourage children to pick up the best of the two cultures. Further research would be required to confirm such a link but at the moment it is enough to suggest that employment influences perceptions of the past and could be a positive factor in bringing up children.

Thus an Asian lady employed as a company secretary in an insurance firm maintained:

> "when we came in initially from Kenya, we lost all our friends but we don't feel that any more – so much goes on culturally."

Another lady who works in an accounting firm felt,

> "At first it was difficult but now there are temples. It is up to us to see which values are important and teach our children to be respectful."

A playgroup worker described her settlement thus:

> "there are bound to be hardships. Settling down is never easy. I encourage my children to do their best in education but at home we speak Gujerati and stick to our traditions."

Models used for coping with concerns

Fifty-one per cent of the females in the sample coped through prayer as opposed to 34 per cent of the males. Fourteen per cent of the females and only 3 per cent of the males would cry. Twice as many males compared to females said they were likely to externalise feelings of distress by rowing with the family or by coping through hard work.

This data draws attention to the fact that women tend to internalise their problems to a greater degree than men and are potentially liable to being affected by their concerns at the emotional level.

It is interesting that some Asian men perceived mental distress as a particularly female experience,

> "women in our community are more likely to experience distress because they tolerate a great deal and don't speak up."

This leads us to consider whether certain concerns affect more or less of one gender. This information could be valuable in designing mental health education for Asian males and females.

Fourteen per cent of men and 19 per cent of women were concerned with the future of their children. Women were more likely to present concerns related to marriage and health (5% and 29%). It is significant that no males presented marital concerns and 11 per cent had worries over health. Employment was a more pressing concern for women (13%) as opposed to 9 per cent in men, but financial worries troubled more men (37%) compared to women (8%).

However, both categories are negatively affected by their concerns to the same degree (37% of males and 38% of females). A substantial proportion of females described the effect in emotional terms (i.e. 20%) as opposed to 6 per cent of males.

Thus the women in our sample were more vulnerable than men at the emotional level when faced with adversity. Women were less able than men to channel concerns into external manifestations such as rowing with the family or coping through hard work. It also shows that mental health issues for Asian males and females vary. These variations must be taken into account when planning mental health services for these categories.

Roles

The most meaningful activity for women surrounded the family. Fifty-seven per cent of the women as compared to 20 per cent of the men pointed to familial responsibilities as most meaningful. Men were more likely to find leisure, business, career or community/voluntary work as more meaningful.

Table 10 – Role Satisfaction for Males and Females

Base. All respondents

Role satisfaction	Total	Male	Female
Total	98	35	63
Yes	70	26	44
No	21	5	16
Don't Know	6	3	3
Not Appl	1	1	0

Twenty-five per cent of females were dissatisfied with roles. A lesser proportion (i.e. 14%) of males held similar notions of their roles.

Table 11 – Reasons for Role Dissatisfaction

Base. All responses

Why dissatisfied	Total	Male	Female
Total	**21**	**5**	**16**
Lack of income	2	1	1
Abused	5	0	5
No Role	1	1	1
Unable to reach expectations	3	1	2
Lack of independence	4	2	2
Not Answered	5	0	5

Thirty-one per cent of females who expressed dissatisfaction over roles were abused and disrespected within the family. Twenty per cent of the males who were dissatisfied were unable to reach the level they had aspired and 40 per cent experienced a lack of independence.

The data on what is considered meaningful activity indicates that women more commonly associate this type of activity with familial responsibilities while men would seek the market model through work business or leisure in order to define activities that are meaningful. Dissatisfaction with roles amongst females is likely to occur when the model of the family is threatened by abuse and disrespect.

Age Differentiation

The sample consisted of the following age profile.

Table 12 – Age differentiation

Base. All respondents

Age	Total
16 - 25	10
26 - 35	25
36 - 45	22
46 - 45	22
56 - 65	14
66 plus	5

In this section we shall highlight some of the variations on account of age differences. Forty per cent of those within the 16-25 age group saw themselves as British and 20 per cent as Asian. Within the 26-35 age band, 56 per cent classified themselves as Asian and only 12 per cent as British. The self-perception of a greater number was Asian within the 36-45 and 46-55 age bands respectively but this is reversed in the 56-65 age band where more people perceived themselves as British.

The educational background of the 16-25 age band was significantly different from the others. A majority had received instruction in this country. Forty per cent had 'O' levels, 10 per cent had CSE and 10 per cent had 'A' levels. Twenty per cent had received a university degree.

Table 13 – Experience in Education for the 16-35 Age Group

Base. All responses who had received part or all of their education in this country.

Responses	Experience in Education		
	Total	16-25	26-35
Total	29	15	14
Positive Comments			
Satisfactory	6	2	4
No Barriers	4	1	3
Advice/ career	6	4	2
None Known	1	0	1
Negative comments			
Language problem	1	1	0
Peer Group	3	1	2
Barriers (Racism)	4	4	0
Lack of career advice	3	2	1
Not Known	1	0	1

Sixty-four per cent of the responses of those in the 26-35 age group were satisfied with the education received. Out of these, 30 per cent said they did not face racism and 22 per cent of the responses related to support from teachers. Within the 16-25 segment, however, only 20 per cent were satisfied but 27 per cent could access good career advice and 13 per cent had not faced racism.

Forty-one per cent of all responses from those born in this country and those immigrated before the age of 16 referred only to negative experiences. The majority of the negative responses (53%) came from the 16-25 group. Twenty-six per cent of the negative responses pointed to racism and 26 per cent to the lack of career guidance and to peer group pressure.

The data indicates a relative decline in positive experiences in education for the 16-25 age group as compared to the 26-35 category. We will now look at the dominant concerns in the different age bands bearing in mind that historical experiences could vary.

Table 14 – Concerns of different age groups

Base. All responses expressing concerns

Concerns Total	Total 98	16-25 10	26-35 25	36-45 22	46-55 22	56-65 14	66+ 5
Children	33	2	8	11	7	3	2
Marriage	5	0	2	1	1	1	0
Financial	18	3	7	2	3	2	1
Employment	11	2	3	4	2	0	0
Education	6	3	2	1	0	0	0
Environment	4	2	1	0	1	0	0
Mugging	8	0	2	1	2	3	0
Poll Tax	4	0	1	2	0	0	1
Health	22	0	5	4	5	6	2
Religion/cult.	4	0	3	0	1	0	0

Thirty per cent of the 16-25 age group expressed concerns relating to education and 20 per cent had environment-related concerns and a further 20 per cent were concerned about children. Thirty per cent experienced financial difficulties.

An eighteen year old Asian girl currently doing her A levels was uncertain about her choice of course,

> *"I am doing A levels in Sociology and Economics. I had wished to do something else but results did not permit. Maybe I should move to Business Studies. I do not want to feel I wasted two years in the end."*

Environmental concerns were relevant for this group. This young person was actively campaigning against the council's proposal to acquire her parents' house and others in the neighbouring area in order to construct roads. According to her,

> *"The council keeps writing on this new proposal. It would be a real upheaval to move out; there's no alternative but to resist this scheme through organised effort."*

It was common for respondents in this category to express finance-related concerns. As one of them said:

> *"Sometimes I am very worried about money. In this country a small amount of money is not enough. I still have to buy a house and get married. This I cannot do without a secure job and sizeable income."*

The major concerns in the 26-35 band were financial problems. Thirty-two per cent were concerned with the future of children, 20 per cent worried over health problems. In the 36-45 age group the most significant concern was over children, 50 per cent expressing concerns about children. Marital concerns affected 5 per cent while 18 per cent were affected by employment and health problems respectively.

Health emerges as a significant problem from 46 years upwards, increasing from 23 per cent for this group to 43 per cent in the 56-65 age group and 40 per cent in the 66 plus.

Effects of Concerns and Coping Mechanisms

The age groups which reported the most concerns ranging from fairly severe to very severe were those in the 46-55 and 56-65 age bands. For both these groups 64 per cent had concerns in these categories. The younger age groups were more likely to report concerns which were either fairly severe or not severe.

Table 15 – Age and Effect of Concerns

Base. All responses on effect of concerns

Age	Total	Negative Effect	Emotional Distress
16-25	10	3	1
26-35	25	7	7
36-45	22	9	6
46-55	22	10	7
56-65	14	7	4
66 +	5	1	1

In the youngest age group (16-25), 30 per cent said they were negatively affected by concerns and a third of these saw this as leading to emotional distress.

Twenty-eight per cent of the 26-35 age group were adversely affected and 100 per cent of these felt this had caused emotional disturbances.

Forty-one per cent in the 36-45 band had negative experiences with concerns and two-thirds of these saw this as affecting emotions. The largest proportion of those negatively affected (50%) were part of the 56-65 age group.

In terms of coping mechanisms likely to be used, 40 per cent of the 16-25 age group would prefer to help themselves, 20 per cent were likely to talk their problems through and 10 per cent would turn to the services.

They were less likely to find a resolution through prayer or family support.

The 26-35 age band were most likely to work hard (24%) in order to change the situation. A majority (41%) of the 36-45 category expressed self-confidence as an effective coping mechanism and 9 per cent would find solace in prayer. Prayer as a means to derive strength was, however, more marked as age advances beyond 46 years.

The youngest age group were the most optimistic and no-one felt they couldn't be helped. They would seek help from the services or outside/ community groups and would resort to self-help where appropriate.

They felt:

> "Without an organisation to back your aims little can be achieved."

> "The right channels need to be approached which is not possible without organised efforts."

Forty per cent of this category were seeking a change in tradition and structure and were prepared to work towards this goal. They were more likely to share political and environmental concerns and many interpreted changes of structure in these terms.

CHAPTER 5

Conceptions of Health & Care

In this chapter we shall explore whether our sample of the Asian community make use of the conventional pathways to care with reference to mental health.

Twenty-eight per cent of responses from the sample reported ways in which existential concerns negatively affected well-being. Out of these 70 per cent described these experiences in emotional terms. Only one, however, considered it necessary or appropriate to make contact with the G.P. for this reason. Instead, contact with the G.P. was made at a point when marked physical symptoms appeared, thus leaving a trail of distress symptoms undetected.

The above evidence raises important questions on the spectrum of normality and pathology in different cultures and challenges some of the formulations used to explain the low rate of reported mental illness in the Asian community. Asians appear to suffer less psychological morbidity than the indigenous population and tend to manifest greater "psychological robustness" (Cochrane & Steptoe 1981). Others have linked this phenomena with stereotypical conceptions such as fear of stigmatisation or fatalistic notions associated with the way Asians conceptualise mental health.

Our data, on the contrary, suggests that emotional difficulties are recognised, for a significant proportion of the sample, but are not classified as pathological. It has been suggested that somatic symptoms are commonly presented by emotionally disturbed patients of Asian origin, leading to a "somatisation" of emotional distress (Rack 1982). This formulation assumes the relevance of western constructs such as the distinction between the mind and the body for people from different cultures. Our data supports the view that knowledge of what is normal and pathological is shaped by cultural definitions of person-hood, social identities and role expectations (See Klienman, Walker, White 1982).

The segment of our sample facing emotional difficulties were less able to compartmentalise this set of experiences as affecting the "individual psyche". Instead, they were more likely to use a holistic model and link such experiences within a normative structure of roles and expectations. Emotions, which are private experiences located within the inner self in individualistic cultures, are often externalised in traditional cultures and located in the relationship between the subject and object of the feeling (Pina Cabral 1986).

Using the general perspective the data has thrown up so far, we shall now enter into a more detailed analysis of health issues and the kind of health problems that are taken to the G.P.

Fifty-seven per cent of the total sample had no problems with health; 27 per cent of those who classified themselves as emotionally distressed did not see their conditions as a health hazard and reported no problems with health.

Forty-one per cent of the sample suffered from poor health. Within this category the majority did not suffer from prolonged illness. However, 36 per cent of the health problems needed continuous medical attention and 12 per cent linked health condition with stress.

Fourteen per cent of the sample suffered from coronary heart disease, blood pressure or diabetes. Eight per cent reported loss of energy and fatigue and 16 per cent experienced aches/pains and arthritis. The majority of the sufferers in the last two categories were women.

Major Causes of Ill-Health

Table 16 – Major Causes of Ill-Health

Base. All respondents reporting poor health

Major Causes	%
Physical/Medical condition	14
Weather	16
Overwork	12
Old age	3
Stress	19
Other	2
No Cause	8
Not Ans.	7
Not applicable	17

If we look closer into those who reported stress as a major cause of ill-health, we discover a link with historical and local experience. Those who had interpreted settlement as unjust and had to cope with cultural and language barriers leading to isolation were more likely to have been through stressful experiences. No one within our sample who had recognised racism and possibly challenged it reported stress. Our data has shown that certain categories of people in employment such as manual labour were less likely to experience racism overtly. Similarly, housewives are relatively cut off from mainstream racist practices. These categories are less able to politicise themselves and challenge racism. Where positive responses to racism are absent, the hierarchy may be seen as immutable, creating conditions where stress is likely to occur.

Life Events, Concerns and Stress

Table 17 – Life events, Concerns and Stress

Base. All respondents who linked poor health with cause

Cause	Total 98	Children 33	Marriage 5	Financial 18	Health 22
Stress	19	6	5	5	3

All concerns relating to marriage were seen as stressful. Fourteen per cent of health-related concerns, 28 per cent of financial concerns and 18 per cent of concerns regarding children were described as causing stress.

Life Events

The association between life event stresses with long term contextual threat and an increased risk of psychological disturbances is now fairly well established (Brown et al 1987, Creed 1988). We shall examine the validity of this association with reference to our data.

Twenty-seven per cent of the sample could link life events with health condition.

Table 18 – Life Events and Health

Base. Respondents whose health was affected by life events

Cause	Total 26	Male 9	Female 17
Death/illness spouse	7	1	6
Unemployment	3	2	1
Miscarriage	2	0	2
Child birth	1	0	1
Separation family/relative	1	1	0
Other	3	2	1
N/A	9	3	6

This lady who was recently widowed described her health thus:

"Since my husband's death, I have been feeling very poorly with dizziness, aches and pains. I feel this has been caused by sorrow and loneliness."

"My husband was seriously ill after by-pass surgery. The tension of helping my husband pull through gave me diabetes. I was fine before that."

Lamenting over his wife's health problem, one informant said:

"I constantly worry over my wife's health. I've had a heart attack and suffer from acute pain in the elbow and seem to have problems with the cartilage as well."

Another lady who had lost her husband a few months after coming into this country developed tuberculosis,

"I have recovered from that but continue to suffer from a consistent pattern of weakness, headaches and dizziness."

A series of miscarriages has left a young mother,

"with no energy. I am exhausted with the routine and repetitiveness of housework. There is in a sense a feeling of constant fatigue."

A father affected by his daughter's poor health conditions maintained:

"The worry of my daughter's condition often causes stomach upsets, lack of sleep, high blood pressure and nausea."

41

Twenty per cent of the sample saw the correspondence between life events and poor health but only 62 per cent of these had taken their complaints to the G.P. Thirty-one per cent of the category who did go to the G.P. had experienced inappropriate treatment. (It is significant that the treatment was seen as inappropriate because only a medical treatment was offered or the treatment lasted for a brief period. In addition, fear of losing confidentiality or not being accurately understood due to communication barriers contributed to a feeling of dissatisfaction with the treatment offered).

Table 19 – Reasons for seeing the G.P. in the past two years

Base. All respondents

Reasons	%
Chest pains	14
Flu/colds	29
Blood Pressure/Stroke/Diabetes	9
Post/anti-natal/Gynaecological	10
Vaccination/Routine check	5
Stress	3
Other	5
Not ans/Not appl.	25

This evidence corroborates our earlier findings that respondents who made the correspondence between concerns and emotional difficulties are not likely to contact the G.P. for these problems. While problems affecting physical health are seen as essentially "individual afflictions" and responsive to a model of medical treatment offered by the G.P. , emotional problems linked to one's life situation are seen in the context of personhood and social roles. The latter are seen to be within the parameters of normality, distinct from "illness" categories implicit within the medical model administered by the G.P.

Three per cent of the sample had seen the G.P. for stress-related problems but a majority of these had concerns linked with children's health. They had accompanied their children on visits to the G.P. and were able in this context to communicate stressful experiences. The data thus suggests that stress-related disturbances are generally not presented to the G.P.

Physical health and the G.P.

The material relating to positive and negative experiences with G.P. treatment refer to physical health and related episodes as these are classified as "illness" within the culture of our sample.

Table 20 – Positive & negative experiences with the G.P.

Base. All responses relating to experiences with the G.P.

Experiences	Total
Positive	
Pleased with G. P.	32
No problems with communication	12
Appropriate diagnosis	6
Others	4
Not answered	10
Negative	
Not pleased with G. P.	4
Problems with communication	6
Inappropriate Diagnosis	3
Others	8
Not answered	9

Twenty-one per cent of the sample had negative experiences with the G.P.

As one man reported:

"The G.P. doesn't want to touch you. He just sits down and hands over prescriptions as if it were an office job."

"The G.P. saw I was losing weight. I was down to seven and a half stone. My cough was so bad but the G.P. seems to think all was well. After we insisted he sent me for a blood-check. My report was mixed up with someone else. I was given the wrong medicine. This made me dizzy. Another G.P. sitting in at the time discovered the mix-up."

Another couple who had been seeing their G.P. for problems relating to the wife's infertility said:

43

> *"We have been seeing the G.P. for a long time. It was only after a great deal of insistence on our part after considerable time had lapsed, that he referred us to a consultant. When major tests were undertaken it was recommended that surgery would be required. By this time, my wife had become totally disillusioned and now refuses to have surgery done."*

The husband of a lady who suffers from severe migraine had this to say about his G.P.:

> *"The G.P. has been reluctant to help. He was unwilling to refer my wife to a consultant and kept on prescribing drugs. I finally had to go private. A head-scan was done. Now a different diet has been recommended and she has been asked not to take any drugs."*

An older person suffering from diabetes and arthritis felt:

> *"The G.P. never sends for a second opinion. He keeps giving medicines that don't help. He says every old person in this country has a problem and we have to learn to put up with it."*

The part of our sample who had experienced emotional disturbances approached the G.P. when physical symptoms begin to appear. The G.P. was not seen as the appropriate person to discuss emotional difficulties. As one of them remarked:

> *"the G.P. has no time for people. Anything he can reckon as physical he treats. I went to the G.P. with aches and pains and was treated for this. He doesn't know anything about my other problems."*

The data draws attention to the need to design services to help those with emotional problems. As we have seen, a major proportion of Asians do not use the conventional pathways to care when faced with emotional difficulties.

CHAPTER 6

Mental Distress

Within this chapter, we attempt to reach an understanding of the way Asian informants themselves define mental distress.

The shift in perspective is likely to raise questions on the validity and measurability of recognisable symptoms. However, this research is not about prevalence rates of mental distress but rather on the ways it is conceptualised and how this might in turn lead to symptoms being undetected. We wish to draw from the data collected mainly individual responses to psychological disturbances and assess how these responses fit into medical models.

"Psychological abnormality is always recognised against a background of particular beliefs about normality which are themselves cultural. Within given biological constraints there is considerable variation in both the presence and the type of psychological expression. This variation is socially determined" (Littlewood & Lipsedge 1982).

We approach these issues by looking at some of the more general relationships between life experiences and distress. Subsequently, some illustrative cases will be used to examine the more specific links.

Age Group Distribution

Table 21. Mental Distress & Age Group Distribution

Base. All respondents who were distressed

Age Range	Total 98	Distressed 22	%
16-25	10	1	10
25-36	25	7	28
36-45	22	4	18
46-55	22	6	27
56-65	14	3	21
66	5	0	0

The age bands 25-36 and 46-55 appear most vulnerable to distress within our sample. The 36-45 and 56-65 age bands follow with 18 per cent and 21 per cent respectively. The youngest age band 16-25 are less vulnerable than the 25- 65 age bands but more vulnerable than the 66 plus age group.

Employment Status and Mental Distress

Table 22 – Employment Status & Mental Distress

Base. Respondents reporting mental distress

Employment status	Total	Mental Distress
Unemployed	13	4
Housewives	28	12
Self-employed	23	5
Student	4	0
Employed	24	1

This data suggests that housewives are more likely to experience emotional distress. Forty-two per cent of our sample of housewives described experiences linked to distress. Students and the employed appear to be less vulnerable. By contrast, almost a third of those unemployed were vulnerable.

Expectations and Settlement

Life experiences constitute significant background factors in determining the migrant's state of mental well-being (Murphy 1977, Littlewood & Lipsedge 1982, McCarthy, Fernando).

Twenty-nine per cent of those who did not find life to be as expected following migration said they were experiencing emotional difficulties.

Table 23 – Different Expectations & Mental Distress

Base. Respondents who found life to be different

Reasons why different	Total	Mental Distress
People/Life unjust	12	4
Culture/Language Difficulties	12	6
Isolation	6	3
Racism	6	1
Weather	6	2
Lack of housing	5	1
Too much hard work	4	1

Those who experienced cultural/language difficulties leading to isolation proved to be most vulnerable to emotional disturbances. A third of those who found the people and life unjust and weather unconducive to settling down reported problems.

Settlement & Mental Distress

Table 24 – Settlement & Mental Distress

Base. All responses of those reporting mental distress

Settlement	Total	Mental distress
Difficulty in preserving culture	21	7
Upbringing children	9	5
Breakdown of family	5	2
Isolation	5	2
Difficulties overcome	15	2
Difficulties in living	5	1
Good infrastructure	4	0
No difficulties	25	3
Preserved Culture	27	2

Difficulties in preserving culture, upbringing of children, disintegration of the family and social isolation appear to be most inimical to mental health. On the other hand, those who were able to overcome initial difficulties or experienced no difficulties in adjusting or in preserving culture and religion reported the lowest rate of mental distress. Professionals need to take these factors into account in diagnosis and counselling.

Coping Mechanisms

Forty-five per cent of the responses from individuals experiencing mental distress reported using "prayer" as a method of dealing with distress. In some cases "prayer" leads to "faith healing" – a mechanism by which intense faith in a religious system or person in the shape of a "guru", "mataji" or "hakim"* helped restore strength and balance to cope with the situation in the person affected.

Within our sample, women who were acutely distressed described the solace brought to them by religious faith. One of these women was being guided by her "guru" to cope with the inter-generational conflicts that characterised her relationship with her children. One of the children had left home and this had caused her acute emotional distress. She blamed herself and felt guilty for what had happened. Her "guru" helped her rationalise the situation and steered her to regain faith in herself.

Another woman suffering from the stressful effect of marital conflict found that things started to be sorted out after her "mataji" endowed her with "special" prayers, that could neutralise the effects of a "curse" which she believed was cast by a member of her husband's family.

A middle-aged woman, who at one point was receiving psychiatric help, said she believed it was prayer that enabled her to abandon medicines and progress towards emotional balance. Four years ago she says she was like a "cabbage." She has had so much healing through faith and prayer that she is coping well with her situation now.

Only 18 per cent of those experiencing mental distress problems were prepared to talk about their problems with a view to seeking help. As mentioned earlier, certain problems were not discussed within the family network. Marital conflicts, for example, are not brought to the family for help and support. On the other hand, health and financial problems were more open to discussion.

---

* *"Gurus", "mataji", "hakim", are spiritual persons who have gained divine knowledge.*

Thirty-six per cent of the same category resorted to crying as a method of coping with distress. Hard work as a method of coping was not used by our sample experiencing mental distress; of those who used this method none reported mental distress problems. By contrast 80 per cent of those who used crying as a way to cope with their situation experienced distress and a third of the sample who believed in "prayer" as a coping mechanism suffered from mental distress.

The data suggests two things; firstly, a substantial proportion of that part of the sample comprising mentally distressed individuals used internal mechanisms such as 'prayer' and 'crying' as a means of dealing with stress. Secondly, we learn that for the sample as a whole, those who were willing to talk about their concerns or work towards overcoming difficult situations were far less vulnerable.

Role Playing & Distress

Out of those who saw themselves as playing a positive role only 10 per cent recorded distress. On the contrary, 90 per cent of those with negated roles classified themselves as distressed. A great proportion of those who saw their roles negatively, associated this view with a loss of meaning connected to the roles. In some cases familial roles were being abused and disrespected. Others felt they were unable to reach expectations associated with their roles, or else there was little scope for challenge and independence within circumscribed roles so that they became repetitive and unmotivating.

Rather than the "individual", it was the social role that was being threatened. This perspective needs to be distinguished from a "mentalistic" model, more common in Western societies where the individual is more likely to be seen as distinct from his/her role. In the Western construct psychological disturbances belong to the domain of the individual causing "illness" – linked to deviation from social norms.

Our respondents, on the other hand, conceptualised distress using a holistic model, where the whole person is affected. When they were asked what changes they would like to see in the next five years, a majority sought a redefinition of roles within the same social contexts. Therefore they did not view distress as "illness" but rather as a condition that signalled an urgent need to restore lost meaning with reference to expected roles.

Perceptions of Mental Distress

It is interesting to record the perceptions of the sample concerning mental distress. Nineteen per cent of the sample associated distress with intra-familial problems, 18 per cent believed that people tend to internalise their problems and this potentially leads to mental distress symptoms. Seventeen per cent viewed social isolation as bringing on distress symptoms and 14 per cent pointed to financial pressures as being particularly disturbing.

Only sixteen per cent of the sample had any idea of how to deal with this problem. On the basis of this evidence it is pertinent to suggest that a major-ity of our sample would potentially use internal mechanisms to cope with these problems if they did occur.

Illustrative Cases

Alok M. is a single male below the age of 25. He has two sisters who live with their grandmother thirty miles away. Alok is therefore alone with his parents, both of whom are working. He came into this country at the age of thirteen. However, the conditions in this country did not meet with his expectations. In India his teaching was in Gujerati which meant that he could not speak or understand English when he arrived.

He entered the state education system but found that language difficulties created severe problems with his peer group and his teachers. He was unable to form any friendships in his school years.

When he joined his school he did not achieve the educational standards required for his age. He was put in a class of younger children who laughed at him and called him "Paki". His negative experiences continued through-out his schooling and at 18 he left school having obtained some 'O' levels.

Alok did not find a job after school and has never since had formal employment. At the same time he started having psychological problems.

Whilst coming across as an intelligent person, Alok describes his emotional and psychological state as being characterised by nervousness, inability to concentrate, sleeplessness and occasional hallucination. He is also losing weight.

Alok was diagnosed as mentally ill and is currently attending a day centre for mentally ill people. At the centre he carries out electrical assembly work.

But Alok does not see himself as a mentally "ill" person and believes he has been misdiagnosed. The real cause of his problems he feels is religious.

Alok is a fairly religious-minded person following the Hindu faith which prohibits the eating of meat. This is significant as Alok feels that his problems are really the work of God who has cursed him for having eaten meat once at school.

Alok, however, prays regularly and uses this as a means of coping with distress as he feels "you become closer to God". He has felt the need to attend temples in the past but there are none in the vicinity.

His treatment in the centre is a major cause of concern to him. Similar to his experience in school he feels he is isolated and has nothing much in common with the other people who attend. He feels he has been put with "mad people", not seeing himself as "mad". He is further isolated as he is the only Asian attending the clinic.

Alok expressed dissatisfaction at the services and felt he was being offered inadequate help. This causes him to feel depressed. He feels the need to talk to people about his feelings but the people cannot understand him. He thinks it would help if he spoke to an Asian social worker.

Retrospectively speaking he wishes he had never come into this country and envisages life to be different in India where he could be part of a network.

Leela S. is a female aged between 26-35. She came into this country from Kenya at the age of eleven. She is now married with one child under the age of three, whom she is very fond of and wishes to see happy.

Although young when she arrived, she was struck by the difference in this country. In this country, she remarked, "no one has time for each other". Her family settled in Leicester. There she joined a local school and did not face any difficulties, as she was taught in English in East Africa.

At school she developed an interest in printing and photography and she was able to make use of the available opportunities to develop this interest and eventually to obtain a vocational qualification in photography. At Leicester she was able to find a job which matched her qualification and interest.

Difficulties started when she got married and moved to live with her husband and his family in London. She found life in London to be difficult and there was "great discrimination over here." Lack of cultural activities and places to go to has meant that she gets so "lonely". This contrasts with her life in Leicester where community links are stronger and she had a network of friends.

Employment opportunities were slim here in London compounded with discriminatory practices. She was never able to find employment and has therefore remained a housewife.

Unfortunately, her role as a housewife is not fulfilling as she is expected to look after her husband's family, clean and cook. She said she, "could go mad doing the same things day after day and would do anything to get out of the house". She describes herself as a lively young person before marriage but now feels there is "nothing to look forward to".

Leela finds it "frustrating" to live with her in-laws, with whom she cannot communicate and is unable to talk about her feelings. She feels her work is not appreciated.

Living with her in-laws has put a strain on her relationship with her husband. She feels her marriage is breaking down as she has continuous arguments with her husband whom she describes as unable to understand her.

Her husband started his own business which has not been very successful. This has put financial pressures on the family. He spends too much time with his business which means he spends less time with his wife.

Although living within a joint family has been problematic, Leela's greatest problem has been her health. She has had four miscarriages. This has affected her emotionally and after the first miscarriage she developed post-natal depression. She has now lost interest in the world around her and finds it difficult to concentrate and remember things. She remarks, "I don't even remember what day it is". Leela sees herself as suffering from mental distress. She has no outlet for her anxieties. She feels she is trapped in family commitment with an unsympathetic husband and "no one to talk to".

Not only was support not available from home but she explains that little help was given from hospital. Her G.P. did not recognise the seriousness of her concern and was not prepared to listen to her, saying that she is young and that there is still a good chance of conception in the future.

"His treatment was disappointing and not convincing." She was not sent to hospital for a consultation.

She would have liked to talk to someone directly after the miscarriages. It is too late now for her to be helped and she feels that she will never get over her concern. Leela persisted, "Can you imagine losing four children? I cannot forget the dates of the children who could be alive." She says she has given up because "there is no hope" and "things can only get worse".

When Leela is depressed she cries and prays for help and "fasting brings some relief inside".

In general she feels that women who experience distress tend "to withdraw socially and they tolerate too much". Expectations from other members of the community can create pressures. People want more than what is required and are very "competitive".

Although Leela presented a very pessimistic picture, she was seeking fresh challenges to her otherwise routine and uninteresting life. She would very much enjoy time spent on leisure activities such as tennis and swimming. She feels she would benefit from mother-toddler groups where she would have someone to talk to.

Aman D. is a middle-aged man. He came to Britain from Bangladesh at the age of 20. In Bangladesh he studied in Bengali up to the school-leaving certificate level. He came into this country to continue his education. However, he experienced many difficulties on arrival. His original intention was to pursue higher education but that had to be abandoned since financial resources were limited and living expenses in this country turned out to be much higher than expected.

Inability to speak English was yet another factor which hindered further education. Aman attended college in the evenings to take ESL classes while the rest of the time he spent working in a restaurant.

Aman found this country to be different in many ways where people are "not particularly friendly and extremely racist".

He is currently self-employed, having left his job to start a business. He is married and has three children aged seven, nine and thirteen. He also has three brothers, one of whom helps him in his shop. However, over the past three years his relationship with his brothers has deteriorated. His wife also does not get on well with her in-laws and this makes it difficult as he "suffers in the middle".

Aman's major worries surround his family and in particular his wife's health. His wife has high blood pressure and is unable to control her bladder for which she requires an operation. She had a thyroid operation in the past and is still receiving medication for this and has to attend regular check-ups. She is described as "suffering from stress and depression" and he feels this is caused by isolation.

Until four years ago his family lived in a council flat where they were harassed by neighbours. This meant his wife did not leave the house much and became extremely depressed. They are now living in their own house which he bought jointly with his brother. In order to buy the house he had to borrow a large sum of money which has meant that financial problems are now quite severe and he is the only person earning in his family.

In addition to his worry over his wife's condition and financial problems he is greatly concerned about his children whom he describes as becoming more and more selfish in this society thinking only of themselves.

The pressure at home has left Aman very stressed. He is "very irritable" and at times feels like "breaking objects in front of him" or "beating the children". He is "unhappy at all times" and "gets no pleasure out of life".

The breakdown of his wider familial relationship and his wife's condition means he has no outlet for his feelings and says that "because I cannot express my feelings I suffer a great deal from keeping it pent up".

Aman sees that there is a link between problems at home and his health. He stated that, "if my wife's condition improves I will have no major problems." He feels she may be helped if one of her sisters came from abroad.

Ten years ago Aman had a heart attack. He also suffers from an acute pain in his elbow. He visited the G.P. for this. However, he explains that the G.P. has given him three injections without explaining the cause. Aman expressed dissatisfaction with the G.P.'s treatment.

Because the family has recently moved to the area, he is not aware of any advice centres that he could use. He feels there is an urgent need for counselling facilities for women who are confined to their homes.

The most important thing in Aman's life is his work which he describes as very challenging especially since the shop "is his own".

Rita K is a female aged 46-55. She came to Britain from India at the age of 20. In India she received her education in English obtaining a school-leaving certificate.

She is now married and has three children over the age of 21. When she came into this country "it was a complete change" for her. "People were very cold, not warm, open or friendly." Although the preservation of culture and religion was important to her, she found that work and financial pressures left little time to devote to other activities. Even now she says that "if I had a chance I would go back to where I came from."

Her first job was as a secretary with responsibility for shorthand and typing. She did not aspire to high achievement in employment, "I wasn't one looking for a high position". She faced no problems at work and feels opportunities were available if she wished to pursue them.

She left her job when her mother passed away. Her mother was living with her when she died. She describes her relationship with her mother as very close and says "the bond is beautiful but when she died the pain was far too much." Her mother was very caring and protective with the children.

The death of her mother left her very distressed. She suffered from a lack of concentration, terrible aches and pains, complete loss of interest, lethargy and became extremely depressed.

Her daughter was of great help to her as she could not move much because of severe pain in her joints. She lost interest in her physical upkeep and would go without food and baths. But for her daughter she would have been left in a bad shape.

At this time, her elder son aged 18 started a course in psychiatric nursing. She describes him as a very gentle person but he had a breakdown.

Rita sees her role as a mother as being very protective and says "our children grew up very protected but when they have to face the real world problems start. I wonder whether I did the right thing?"

Her son would "sit in the house like a cabbage" and sometimes he would become extremely aggressive. He was taken to the doctors who prescribed some drugs but he wouldn't take them. He was also taken to a 'Hakim' whose medical preparations did not work either.

Although her husband tried hard to help their son, he was most reluctant to make use of the services. He did not wish to have "anything on record".

They sent his son to live in rented accommodation as they felt this would give him a sense of independence and he would then be able to sort himself out. But this didn't work well either and he would return home to live with his parents. This condition lasted for 9 years. He has now "snapped out of it" and his condition has improved. He has a job and is married with a child.

Rita had, "no support at all. We have no family here. Even the doctor would not make any decisions for you". She visited the G.P. on several occasions with severe arthritis. However, she feels that "G.P.s never have time for people. Anything they reckon as physical they treat. I went to the G.P. with aches and pains and was treated for this."

Now she is able to recognise that her physical symptoms "were all symptoms of depression but at that time I did not know what was happening to me".

With no "real source of help" available she was able to overcome her depression and cope with her son's problems by turning to God and praying. She saw this "as her main anchor". Through "faith healing, a lot of beautiful things happened to me".

Although she is aware of the services and how to use them she feels "they are no good". She has instead drawn courage from faith.

Sanjay is an unemployed Asian male who migrated into this country at the age of eight with his parents. He describes his experience in education as "happy". He had no problems with his friends in school.

Yet he remembers feeling very lonely as his parents had settled in an area where there were virtually no Asians. At the same time his parents were not in favour of his mixing with white children. This left him with no friends of his own age. He feels he was never able to "integrate" as the choice was between "isolating oneself from the mainstream or forgetting one's own culture".

He grew up feeling in the "middle of nowhere". However, after the completion of school he trained as a computer engineer and found a suitable job.

Having worked for ten years, "personal problems" forced Sanjay to leave his job. The problem he maintained was not linked with the work itself as he was satisfied with his job. Problems arose at the social level which he says resulted from his parents' not "permitting me to mix with English children".

He feels he ought to have "sorted his life out at an early stage". When he started having psychological problems and this affected his work he approached his G.P.

Sanjay was able to take his problems to the G.P. and present these problems in psychological terms. Sanjay had received all his education and professional training in this country and this possibly is one reason why he was able to use the conventional route to psychiatric care.

Sanjay's emotional problems were presented to the G.P. with symptoms such as "my brain's going around in circles". The G.P. is closely monitoring his progress and gives him medication whenever it is necessary.

Throughout this unhappy experience his family has been unable to understand his dilemma. He has had no support at all from his family. They are aware of how he feels but "sometimes they want to help and sometimes they don't".

He is not in a position to go back to work at the moment as he is unable to "retain an interest in anything constructive".

Yet he hopes he will go back to work as soon as it is possible and sees that "there is a very good chance of this happening".

Sanjay is knowledgeable of the services and is aware of how to use them. He is currently using the psychological services to rehabilitate himself and return to work.

Meena came into this country from Mauritius at the age of 23 to join her husband whom she had married in Mauritius. It was a marriage that was arranged by both the families.

When she came into this country she was "very lonely" and longed to go back. Her husband did not have a house of his own so they lived with his sister in a house that belonged to her. This arrangement was something for which she was not prepared.

Initially her marriage was very good when she describes her husband as "supportive and wonderful". But soon, her sister-in-law turned hostile and suspicious. This created a great deal of tension between her husband and herself. Her husband's loyalties changed and gradually he began to side with his sister. Meena was isolated in a little room of the house and was not allowed to go out or even write to her family back in Mauritius.

Even after she had her son the situation did not improve. She wondered why her husband who so much wanted a son initially had begun ill-treating her. He gave her no money. He had turned violent and unfeeling.

With no support at all from the family she felt "powerless" and there was "little she could do".

The "stress" in her life and experience in marriage caused her physical problems. She explains that she could not eat or sleep. She suffered from aches and pains and lost interest in everything. "I did not feel like dressing, working or doing anything." When all this was happening her husband "was never bothered" about her health.

Meena approached the G.P. when her physical problems began escalating. The G.P. would prescribe pain killers and sleeping pills but "never bothered to find out what the real problem was".

Meena gradually lost "complete faith" in the G.P. and his medicines. Eventually she stopped taking all the tablets as she felt that they were not helping her in any way.

The only thing left between herself and her husband was her son. She says, "it was only my son who gave me a reason to live".

However, as the situation deteriorated she contacted a friend. At this time she even contemplated suicide. Her friend took her to a "Mataji".

The belief was that her sister-in-law had performed "black magic" so that a rift is created in the marriage.

The "Mataji" endowed her with special prayers in order to neutralise the effects of the curse. Ever since, she says she has "regained strength". Her faith in "mataji" has enabled her to cope with her problems and now she feels she has been "saved".

Meena now spends a great deal of her time with her children, whom she says have been very supportive. It is through prayer that she has been able to cope. She continues to pray and finds this to be the most meaningful activity in her life.

Meena now feels she has come to terms with her situation. Her view of the world is more "hopeful". She also sees herself as "physically fit".

In general she maintains that mental distress in women is primarily due to domestic problems. "If this front is all right then you can fight all other problems".

Meena has little faith in the services and says they are there for "publicity", but she feels that there is an urgent need for services for the housebound and some place or context for them to talk.

Usha is a young girl in her teens currently studying for her 'A' levels. Usha was born in this country, her parents having migrated here from East Africa.

At school she experienced racism and says, "directly or indirectly I was made to feel different".

Her major worries concern her education and she feels this is partly due to excessive parental pressure. She is now studying for 'A' levels in Sociology and Economics. She had wished to do other subjects "but her results did not permit it". At the same time Usha doesn't want to feel she has wasted two years in the end.

Usha would like to move to Business Studies which is more practically orientated but "lacks the courage to do so" since her parents expect her to finish 'A' Levels.

Her family continues to treat her as a child. At the same time they have very high expectations of her. Her older sister was always given all the responsibility while she was never taken seriously.

Usha wants her parents to be proud of her but is unable to talk her problems through with her parents. Recently her father has changed jobs and this has brought them closer together.

Usha relies on the advice of her college staff who she feels can "evaluate her potential" better. Whenever she cannot get through to her parents she feels distressed and has difficulty in concentrating. This she feels has affected her health and she is continuously worried about putting on weight. Recently she has lost three stone.

Dieting for Usha has become somewhat obsessive and whenever she is under stress she hardly eats and withdraws. This situation sometimes lasts for as long as a week during which time she does not speak to anyone. Instead she locks herself in a room and consumes bottles of coke. She manages to pull herself together in about a week's time.

Usha doesn't have the confidence to talk to her G.P. who is a friend of the family and her mother normally accompanies her on her visits to the G.P.

Generally Usha feels that the younger generation is under pressure because of arranged marriages. Most of Usha's school friends she describes, "have been forced into marriage".

CHAPTER 7

Uptake of Services

There has been general concern on the low uptake of statutory services by the Asian community. This chapter raises some of the issues surrounding the perception, awareness and use of the services in order to broaden the understanding of the problem.

Awareness of services

It is significant that 32 per cent of the sample were not aware of any of the statutory services.

Eleven per cent of the sample had listed the G.P. while in fact 90 per cent of the sample had used this service. It is difficult to conclusively say why this might be so but one reason may be that the G.P. is not seen by the majority as part of the wider service network: the service is approached for physical problems that are seen as requiring medical treatment. Thus the G.P. service which offers only a medical cure is not seen as appropriate for discussing emotional or social problems.

Six per cent of the sample were aware of social workers and health visitors and a further 6 per cent of mother-toddler groups. Ten per cent had knowledge of statutory advice centres and social security offices. A larger proportion, 15%, identified citizens' advisory bureaux. The majority, 21%, however, demonstrated awareness of the services provided by Asian voluntary agencies.

Table 25 – Information on Services

Base – All responses

| Information | Total | Country of origin | | | |
		Bangladesh	India	Pakistan	Other
Total	98	14	74	7	3
CABs	19	5	11	2	1
Libraries	12	1	11	0	0
Careers	2	0	1	0	1
Soc Security	26	2	21	3	0
Others	1	0	1	0	0
Don't know	2	0	2	0	0
Not ans	33	5	27	1	0
Not appl	3	1	0	1	1

Table 26 – Use of Services according to Country of origin

Base. All responses – Use of services

| Service Use | Total | Country of origin | | | |
		Bangladesh	India	Pakistan	Other
Total	98	14	74	7	3
None	30	7	23	0	0
GP/HV	13	1	10	1	1
Soc/worker	3	0	2	1	0
Stat/agencies	13	0	11	2	0
Civic Centres	2	0	2	0	0
Asian Vol Org	6	1	4	1	0
Mother-Toddler	3	1	1	0	1
Not Ans	24	4	19	1	0
Not Appl	10	1	5	3	1

The above two tables show the information and use of services on the basis of country of origin. The list of services recorded in the tables represent the selection made by the informants, which means that services that were not represented in the tables were not within the knowledge of the informants.

A comparison between information available and use of the services shows that 62 per cent of the sample as a whole were informed about a part or whole of the services, while only 40 per cent indicated using these services. Thirty per cent of the sample had used none of the services, except perhaps the G.P. service. The highest proportion of non-users were members of the Bangladeshi community. Seven out of the 14 respondents from this category had not used any of the services.

In terms of information, Bangladeshis were better informed about CABs (36%), libraries (7%) and social security benefits (14%) but information on careers and education had failed to reach our sample of Bangladeshis.

For the sample as a whole 15 per cent of the sample had experience with the statutory advice centres, 14 per cent used the G.P. and 6 per cent were in contact with the Asian voluntary sector. Thus the data shows that a very small portion of the sample were in fact utilising the services provided by the voluntary sector in Haringey.

Table 27 – Use of Services and Gender

Base All males and females using the services

Use of services	Total	Male	Female
Total	**98**	**35**	**63**
None	30	10	20
GP/HV	13	3	10
Soc/worker	3	1	2
Stat/Agencies	13	2	11
Civic Centres/Police	2	0	2
Asian Vol Org	6	1	5
Mother-toddler	3	0	3
Not Ans	24	12	12
Not Appl	10	6	4

This table sets out use of services by males and females in the sample. Thirty-two per cent of the females used none of these services. More females (16%) than males (9%) reported using the G.P. or the health visitor.

Seventeen per cent of females and 6 per cent of males had experience with the statutory advice agencies. Mother-toddler groups and police services were utilised by 5 per cent and 3 per cent respectively of the females but there were no males in the sample who had listed using these services. The Asian voluntary sector appeared to be better used by women (3%) than men (8%).

This data reveals that a degree of variation based on gender exists in the uptake of specific services and women tend to access certain services more than men.

Table 28 – Barriers to using Services

Base All responses

What prevents using services	Total	Male	Female
Lack of time	5	2	3
Communication Barriers	29	6	23
Language Barriers	11	4	7
Bad past experience	4	0	4
Adequate family support	2	0	2
Didn't feel the need	14	6	8
Others	1	1	0
Nothing	14	3	11
Not Ans/Not Appl	33	15	18

Fourteen per cent of the responses suggested there were no barriers experienced in accessing services. Another 14 per cent did not feel the need to use services. Of those who said the services were difficult to access, 11 per cent had experienced language barriers. The majority, 29 responses, mentioned problems in communication arising from a lack of confidentiality and trust.

Table 29 – Services that are lacking

Base All responses from those who found the services to be lacking.

Services that are lacking	Total
Statutory services	
Transport/dial-a-ride	9
Asian female doctors/soc workers	10
Outreach workers	4
Better amenities/ Adult education	12
Services for the Housebound	11
Low cost creche	2
Not Ans/Not Appl	59

Forty-five per cent of the responses identified the following statutory services as lacking. Of those who felt the need to improve services in the statutory sector, 19 per cent indicated the need for transport and dial-a-ride for the elderly. Twenty-three per cent wanted services for the housebound. Twenty-one per cent of the responses referred to the need for more Asian female doctors and social workers, while 8 per cent said they would benefit from outreach workers. Twenty-five per cent sought better amenities and opportunities for adult education.

Within the voluntary sector there emerged a marked need for religious and leisure centres (14%) and language and religious classes for children (21%).

Thus although 21 per cent of the sample were aware of the Asian voluntary sector, its services were only used by 6 per cent of the sample.

CONCLUSION

This research aimed to bring together the views of members of the Asian community. Although differences exist within the community, enough similarities were expressed to be able to present a coherent picture of beliefs and concepts of mental health.

In the past researchers have suggested that the prevalence of mental health problems is low within the Asian community. The reasons given are that Asians tend to be psychologically more robust since strong familial and community ties bring about emotional security, also fear of stigmatisation and fatalistic beliefs prevent distress problems being defined as pathological.

This view is challenged by this report which shows the disturbing evidence of the high rate of mental distress problems among the sample studied. Within this randomly selected group of people there was little evidence of psychological robustness or fatalistic attitudes.

The research was based on the assumption that psychological expression of emotional problems is socially determined, shaped by belief systems and cultural definitions which exist within the communities. The spectrum of normality and abnormality varies across cultures and so is the classification of what is viewed as pathological.

The report moves away from western medical models and constructs and presents an alternative approach to understanding the mental health problems of the Asian community.

The sample of this research largely constituted a migrant group. It was found that historical factors and life experiences played a significant part in mental well-being. A tentative link was drawn between life events stresses and long term mental health conditions.

Our sample expressed several concerns, some of which are shared by the indigenous population such as those related to finance and health. However, a significant number of concerns differ from those of the indigenous population and at the same time may not be concerns which would affect the same group if they were in the countries from which they migrated. Hence stereotypes and definitions used in the country of origin cannot be transposed to migrants here, as this group has responded to social processes specific to this country. For example, over 50 per cent of our sample expressed concerns about preserving culture and this often filtered into their concerns over children whom they felt were exposed to external factors often alien to their Asian culture.

Stress was more often reported by those who had migrated singly and did not form part of established networks. This group experienced difficulty with their initial settlement, especially if expectations were not met or if they faced adversity upon arrival. Language problems and cultural differences proved difficult for some, often leading to isolation with subsequent emotional repercussions.

However, not all those who reported concerns were emotionally or physically affected by them. It was only those concerns that were severe and affected individuals negatively that produced emotional disturbances. Certain groups were identified to be more vulnerable. As mentioned above those who experienced settlement problems were more vulnerable. This was particularly so for housewives who were more likely to be isolated and experience difficulty because of cultural differences . Women experiencing marital conflict, reported feelings of powerlessness and were identified as the group most vulnerable to emotional problems. Similarly those women who experienced a loss of meaning in their role because of disrespect and abuse linked this to emotional and physical problems. It was often the case that these problems were internalised and dealt with using internal mechanisms such as prayer and crying.

Among men who reported concerns, emotional disturbances resulted from feelings of powerlessness often expressed by our sample of unemployed men and those who had experienced racism. However, men were better able to cope with emotional problems as they were able to externalise their emotions by rowing or using hard work to diffuse negative feelings.

A significant finding for both Asian men and women was that some existential concerns proved inimical to psychological well-being and led to emotional disturbances. A link was established between life events and poor health. However, many people in our sample did not consult the G.P. even with physical problems as it was felt that G.P.s did not detect the underlying distress symptoms.

However, unlike other research this data does not suggest that Asians somatise emotional distress. Our sample were less able to compartmentalise experiences affecting the individual psyche. They were more likely to use a holistic model and link such experiences within a normative structure of roles and expectations. Distress was therefore conceptualised using a holistic model where the whole person was affected. It was not seen as "illness", but a condition that signalled an urgent need to restore lost meaning with reference to expected roles. In contrast, physical health problems are seen as "individual afflictions" and are responsive to medical treatment as offered by the G.P.

Unfortunately, although our sample recognised the emotional and physical effects that certain stresses and concerns were causing, there were few avenues to express these emotions. Help was only sought from those organisations and individuals who shared a similar cultural background and were able to understand and interpret information presented and offer advice or counselling in a form which was culturally and or religiously appropriate, maintaining a framework of confidentiality.

The low uptake of statutory services within the Asian community calls into question the appropriateness of the existing services. There is a need to move away from stereotypes and over-generalisations and start from the user's frame of reference, taking account of family dynamics, belief systems and cultural constraints.

A number of barriers were identified by our sample with regard to use of available services. The most prominent barriers were problems with communication, lack of knowledge of the services and lack of confidentiality and trust.

This research exposes the urgent need for all those concerned with mental health services for ethnic minorities to take positive action to eradicate these barriers.

SUMMARY OF FINDINGS

Local & Historical Background

1) This research on Mental Health in the Asian Community relates to a largely immigrant population, 80 per cent of whom perceive themselves culturally as Indian, Pakistani or Bangladeshi. Given this, the experience of migration and settlement provide important background material for the understanding of mental health issues in the Asian community.

2) Of those who were satisfied with the settlement conditions in this country the majority were Asian immigrants from East Africa. As twice immigrants they viewed migration in more tangible terms. The pattern of collective immigration provided networks and a cultural continuity that enabled these immigrants to overcome the initial difficulties of settlement. Asian immigrants from the sub-continent, by contrast, were not part of an established network which led to isolation and difficulties with preservation of culture. Poor living conditions linked to housing, weather and social harassment proved insurmountable to a large number of these immigrants who felt betrayed as their expectations were not met.

3) For the sample as a whole, 44 out of the 98 informants did not find this country as expected. Almost a fifth of these outlined differences in living conditions. The rest found it difficult to come to terms with cultural differences arising from unpleasant and unjust attitudes within the dominant culture.

4) However, the experiences relating to cultural differentiation were interpreted in accordance with the present life situation of the informant. Employment status, for example, played a critical part in the interpretation. The unemployed segment of the sample related experiences of racism and unjust treatment. Housewives were more affected by cultural disparities arising from language and communication barriers. The employed viewed settlement in terms of discrimination experienced at work. Culture was not seen as an impediment by a majority of the students within our sample.

Our data suggests that those who maintained cultural bonds and community links were better able to cope with the challenges of the new society.

Employment

5) Forty-five per cent of the sample over the age of 16 were unemployed. Unemployment was less (24%) for the section of the sample born here or arrived before the age of 16.

6) A majority of those in employment, (ie 54%) were in manual work, 21 per cent in semi-skilled and 25 per cent in skilled professions. Twenty per cent of the responses from employed category referred to negative experiences in employment. However, the data suggests that those in manual work were more likely to experience racism indirectly manifested in unacceptable working conditions, job insecurity, low pay and little or no opportunities for mobility. Since racism worked its way indirectly, these people were less able to politicise their experiences in order to challenge racism, leaving them powerless to change their life situation.

7) The responses from those in skilled and semi-skilled work indicated a more overt experience of racism and greater determination to bring about a change in the work situation.

Major Concerns and Models for Coping

8) The major concerns expressed by the sample related to employment, marriage, children, finance and health. A majority of marriage and employment-related concerns were seen by the respondents to be of a severe nature. Twenty-seven per cent of health concerns and 12 per cent of concerns relating to children were considered severe, while only a sixth of financial concerns fell into this category.

9) Those with employment and marriage-related problems had the most severe concerns and were thus more likely to feel entrapped and powerless. A fifth of those with marital problems and more than half with employment problems saw their situation to be irreversible as they believed they could not be helped.

10) Thirty-seven per cent of the 81 in our sample experiencing major concerns were negatively affected by them and 70 per cent of these made the link between the negative effect from concerns and emotional disturbances such as lack of concentration, sleeplessness, excessive tension and a feeling of nervousness.

11) Our data suggests that some support networks are seen as more accessible than others for certain problems. Only 13 per cent of the responses

saw the family as a durable support structure and family networks were used for support relating to health and child care. Support from the services was seen as accessible only by 3 per cent of the responses. Thirty-two per cent of the responses said they would seek help from the voluntary sector provided this was appropriate.

12) Given that on the one hand the family network is not considered appropriate for help with marriage and employment problems and on the other the statutory services are accessed by a negligible portion of the sample, a major gap exists in the support available to Asians experiencing severe concerns. For example, marital conflict and employment problems were more likely to be seen as irreversible and at the same time least likely to be helped.

13) Within the sample a greater proportion preferred to internalise their problems using coping mechanisms such as prayer and crying; 18 per cent of the responses indicated they were able to cope through self confidence and 9 per cent were more pragmatic and used hard work as a means of overcoming difficulties.

Gender and Age Differentiation

14) Although both Asian men and women are disproportionately represented in manual work, more women in our sample have had to continue at these levels for lack of other options. The greatest barriers were experienced by those women who entered employment late.

15) As far as perceptions on migration were concerned, the males within our sample were more likely to link their experiences with problems of race and power leading to inequality; while females were initially at least most affected by the chasm between the two cultures leading to isolation.

16) More women who were unemployed had difficulties in bringing up their children as compared to those in employment. Further research is required to confirm this link but it is tenable to suggest that greater isolation experienced by unemployed women inhibits the development of a broader world view required to cope with intergenerational conflict.

17) Marital concerns are less likely to affect males, while within our sample a considerable proportion of females reported problems with marriage.

18) The same proportion of men and women were negatively affected by concerns, but 20 per cent of the females and only 6 per cent of males

described the effect in emotional terms. This data suggests that women are more vulnerable to emotional distress than men. Males were more likely to externalise distress and use this as a method of coping while a greater proportion of females used internal mechanisms to cope with distress.

19) More women expressed dissatisfaction with roles which they defined using the model of the family. By contrast, men located roles within a market model related to work, business and leisure. Since female roles were linked fundamentally to the family, they were more vulnerable to suffer from abuse and disrespect arising out of role conflicts within the family.

20) In the 16-25 age group the main concerns were education, environmental and financial issues. Those in the 26-35 age band were more affected by children and financial problems, while concerns relating to children also featured prominently in the 36-45 age band. From the age of 46 years and upwards the major concern was health.

21) In the youngest age group, only 10 per cent of those negatively affected by concerns saw this as leading to emotional distress. They were at the same time most likely to help themselves or seek support from statutory and community services.

22) Forty per cent of those in the 16-25 age category were seeking a change in tradition and structure. Since this group was likely to share political and environmental concerns, many interpreted changes of structure in these terms.

23) The age group most vulnerable to mental distress was the 26-35 age category whose concerns surrounded children and finance. Twenty-eight per cent of this group said they were adversely affected by concerns and 100 per cent of these believed this had caused emotional disturbances.

Conception of Health Care

24) Our data establishes that a substantial number of those negatively affected by life concerns are able to link this to emotional disturbances. Yet the low rate of reported mental distress in the Asian community raises questions on how mental health is perceived. Some of the literature explains this phenomenon in terms of greater "psychological robustness" among Asians. Others have used stereotypical conceptions such as fear of stigmatising that leads to suppression of emotional problems.

71

25) The spectrum of normality and pathology is different for the Asian community. From our data it is plausible to suggest that since a distinction is not made between the 'mind' and the 'body' within the Asian cultures, emotional distress is seen as affecting the 'person' rather than the 'individual'. Consequently, emotional disturbances are not 'pathological' as is commonly assumed in the western medical model.

26) Physical illnesses are seen as individual afflictions and thus fit for medicalisation. But emotional problems connected with social roles and the "collective" are seen to lie within the boundaries of 'normality'. These problems are taken to the G.P. at the point when physical symptoms begin to appear.

27) Thus a good deal of time passes when emotional stress is undetected. When they are presented to the G.P. as physical symptoms it is likely that the underlying link with the 'psyche' is missed in the diagnoses.

Mental Distress

28) Forty-two per cent of the women who were unemployed reported distress. Employment was seen as a positive factor for mental health. A third of those whose initial settlement experiences led to a belief that people and life were unjust experienced emotional distress. But 50 per cent of the category experiencing cultural and language differences leading to isolation were vulnerable to emotional problems.

29) The lowest rate of mental distress were reported by those who were able to preserve culture through established networks.

30) Ninety per cent of those who saw their roles as negated experienced distress. Roles were negated in several ways. For example, role conflicts within the family led to abuse and disrespect. Sometimes role expectations were not being reached or else there was a lack of motivation to perform repetitive roles.

At the same time amongst those who saw themselves as playing positive roles only 10 per cent reported mental distress.

31) When internal mechanisms were used for coping with concerns, it was likely to result in psychological disturbances. However, when "faith healing" was tried through the vehicle of a holy person such as "Guru", "Mataji" or "Hakim" vulnerable individuals experienced a restoration of inner strength and hope.

32) The data shows that amongst those who were able to discuss and talk through their concerns, or used self confidence and hard work as a method of coping with concerns, no one reported mental distress.

Uptake of Services

33) Thirty-two per cent of the sample were unaware of the services provided by the local authority other than that of the G.P. Although ninety per cent of the sample were aware of the G.P., only 11 per cent saw this as a service.

34) Thirty per cent of the sample had not used any of the services other than that of the G.P. The highest proportion of non-users were from the Bangladeshi community. Out of the 14 respondents within our sample, 7 had not used any of the services.

35) There is little awareness of where to go for emotional and social problems. Thus only 6 per cent of the sample were aware of the social workers.

36) The greatest barriers surrounding the low uptake of services were linked to communication problems, lack of confidentiality and trust and inadequate knowledge of the services, leading to powerlessness and a lack of faith.

37) Forty-five per cent of the responses identified statutory services as lacking. Of those who wanted to see an improvement in statutory services, 19 per cent indicated the need for transport, 23 per cent wanted services for the housebound, 25 per cent sought better facilities for adult education and 21 per cent said they would benefit from being treated by Asian doctors/social workers.

RECOMMENDATIONS

- Experience of migration, settlement & life-expectations provide important background material that must be taken into account in the assessment of mental health of immigrant communities.

- Awareness of variations in people's interpretations of the past arising from factors such as unique historical events or current life situations could potentially lead to a better understanding of some of the epidemiological factors underlying mental distress.

- Planning of mental health services for the Asian community should consider the different needs based on gender and age differentiations, so that services are more responsive to the transformations within this community.

- The report highlights the urgent need to move away from stereotypes and over-generalisations. Constructs such as "stigma" or "fatalism" commonly used to characterise the alleged "suppression" of mental distress must be challenged.

- The data raises the need to redefine the spectrum of "normality" and "pathology" for different cultures. These conceptions must be incorporated into a pattern of diagnosis and treatment within psychiatric care.

- It is time to consider that mental distress could remain unreported because medicalisation is not seen as appropriate to deal with distress. Conventional pathways to psychiatric care are less often used by the Asian community. Statutory services must target at the "undetected" phase in the experience of stress.

- More training is needed to raise awareness of health professionals on acceptable methods to approach social and emotional problems experienced by people in different communities. Training must take into account areas such as improving communication based on understanding the person's own formulation of his/her mental health. This could lead to developing a system of care that does not categorise or de-humanise.

- Mental Health Education needs to disseminate material targeted at different age and gender groups, such that they are more appropriate to the concerns and coping models likely to be used by these categories.

- Positive coping mechanisms used to deal with stress must be incorporated both into Mental Health Education as well as provide a framework for counselling and support services.

- There is an urgent need to design support services with the skills and framework of confidentiality that could meaningfully respond to the major concerns experienced by the Asian community. In order to do this it would be important to develop a pattern of care that does not endanger the models of mental health used by the community.

- Counselling services should be directed at areas where there is greatest need. Marital problems, for instance, could be helped by developing a pattern of family therapy appropriate to these communities.

- Health services should respond positively to the barriers linked to poor communication and powerlessness that account for the low uptake of services in the Asian community.

- The report raises the importance of targeting training and education at unemployed Asian women in order to enable them to return to work. As our data illustrates, this category is most vulnerable to mental distress and at the same time employment works as a positive factor in mental health.

- The findings also highlight the need to develop services targeted at the elderly and housebound, and to improve the representation of Asian female doctors, social workers and outreach workers within the services.

Bibliography

Bagley, C. The Social Aetiology of Schizophrenia in Immigrant Groups. *International Journal Social Psychiatry*. Vol. 17, No 4. 1971.

Bagley, C. Mental Health in Immigrant Minorities in London. In Verma.G. (ed). *Race and Education across Cultures*. 1971.

Bebbington, P.E. *et al* Psychiatric Disorders in Selected Immigrant Groups in Camberwell. Social Psychiatry. Vol. 16, No 1. 1981.

Burke, A.W. Racism & Psychological Disturbance among West Indians in Britain. *Transcultural Psychiatry*. Vol. 30, 1984.

Burke, A.W. Is Racism a Causatory Factor in Mental Illness? *International Journal of Social Psychiatry*. Vol. 30, 1 & 2 1984.

Burke, A.W. Psychic Function and Mental Stress: The Ethnic Minority Population. *In* Allen S. Stacey M. (*eds*) *Race & Social Policy*. 1988.

Carpenter, L. & Brockington I.F. A Study of Mental Illness in Asians, West Indians & Africans Living in Manchester. *British Journal of Psychiatry*. Vol. 137, 1980.

Carstairs, G.M. Some Problems of Psychiatry in Patients from Alien Cultures. Lancet. 1985.

Caines, R. The Cultural Factors in Mental Health. In *Social Work Today*.Vol. 17 1986.

Cochrane, R. & Steptoe, M. Psychological & Social Adjustment of Asian Immigrants to Britain: A Community survey. *Social Psychiatry* Vol. 12, 1977.

Costin, Larry. Racial Minorities & the Mental Health Act. *Mind Out*. Vol. 49, 1981.

Cox, J.L. Medical Management, Culture & Mental Illness. *British Journal of Hospital Medicine*. Vol. 27, No 5, 1982.

Fernando, S.J.M. *Race & Culture in Psychiatry*. Croom Helm. 1988.

Fernando, S.J.M. A Cross-Cultural Study of some Familial & Social Factors in Depressive Illness. *British Journal of Psychiatry*. Vol. 127, 1975

Fernando, S.J.M. Depressive illness in Jews & Non Jews. *British Journal of Psychiatry*. Vol. 112, 1966.

Goffman, E. *Asylums*. Penguin Books. London. 1971.

Hashmi, Farrukh. Community Psychiatric Problems among Birmingham Immigrants. *British Journal of Psychiatry*. Vol. 2, 1986.

Jervis, M. Female, Asian & Isolated. *Open Mind.* Vol. 2, 1986.

Khandwalla, M. A Specialist Community Care Psychiatric Service of Ethnic Minorities. *Community Psychiatric Nursing Journal,* Vol. 5, 1985.

Kingsley, S. The Mental Health of Ethnic Minorities in London. GLC. *Mental Health Services in London.* 1984.

Kleinman, A.M. Concepts & a Model for the Comparison of Medical Systems as Cultural Systems. *Social Science & Medicine.* Vol. 12, 1978.

Kleinman, A.M. Depression, Somatisation & the New Cross Cultural Psychiatry. Social Science & Medicine. Vol. 11, 1977.

Leff, J. Culture & Differentiation of Emotional States. *British Journal of Psychiatry.* Vol. 24, 1973.

Littlewood, R. Anthropology & Psychiatry – An Alternative Approach. *Journal of Medical Psychiatry.* Vol. 53 , 1980.

Littlewood, R. *Aliens and Alienists – Ethnic Minorities and Psychiatry.* Penguin. London. 1982.

London, M. Mental Illness Amongst Immigrant Minorities in the United Kingdom. *British Journal of Psychiatry.* Vol. 149, 1986.

McCarthy, B. & Craissati, J. Ethnic Differences in Response to Adversity. *Social Psychiatry.* Vol. 24 1989.

McNaught, A. *Race & Health Care in the United Kingdom.* Occasional Paper No 2. Health Education Council. 1985.

Malik, Farah. Asian Women, Mental Health & Mental Ill Health. *The Myth of Mental Illness.* Asha (Southwark) 1986.

Malzberg, B. & Lee, E.S. Migration & Mental Disease. *Social Science Research Council.* New York 1956.

Marsella, A.J. Depressive Affect & Disorder Across Cultures. *In* H.Triandis & J.Draguns (eds) *Handbook of Cross Cultural Psychology.*Vol. 5, New Jersey: Allyn & Bacon 1979.

Marsella, A.J. Cross-Cultural Studies of Mental Disorders. *Perspectives on Cross-Cultural Psychology.* 1979.

Mercer, Kabena. Black Communities' Experience of Psychiatric Services. *International Journal of Social Psychiatry.* Vol. 30, 1984.

Murphy, H.B. Migration Culture & Mental Health. *Psychological Medicine.* Vol. 7, 1977.

Murray, J. & Williams, P. Self-reported Illness & General Practice Consultations in Asian-Born Residents of West London. *Social Psychiatry.* Vol. 21, 1989.

Pina, J. Cabral. *Sons of Adam, Daughters of Eve: The Peasant World View in Alto Minho.* Oxford: Clarendon Press 1986.

Rack, P. *Race Culture & Mental Disorder*: Tavistock. London 1982.

Rack, P. Diagnosing Mental Illness. Asians & the Psychiatric Services. *In* Khan Verity (*ed*) *Minority Families in Britain. Support Services & Stress.* MacMillian 1979.

Runneymede Trust. Mental Health & Racism. *Race & Immigration* Vol. 158, 1983.

Walker. N.E. Culture & Mental Illness. *The Journal of Nervous & Mental Disease.* Vol. 159, 1974.

Ward, L. Racism & Mental Health in Britain. *Radical Community Medicine.* No 34, 1988.

White, G.M. The Ethnographic Study of Cultural Knowledge of Mental Disorder. *In* Marsella.A.J.& White.G.M (*eds*) *Cultural Conceptions & Mental Health & Therapy.* 1982.

Whitehead, M. *The Health Divide: Inequalities in Health in the 1980s.* Health Education Council 1987.

Zola, I.K. Pathways to the doctor – from person to the patient. *Social Science & Medicine.* Vol. 7, 1973.

Appendix 1: Residents born in Asia, New Commonwealth & Pakistan by ward

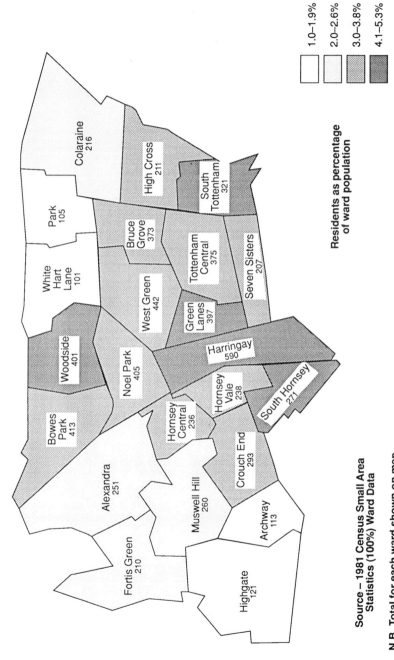

Residents as percentage of ward population

- 1.0–1.9%
- 2.0–2.6%
- 3.0–3.8%
- 4.1–5.3%

Colaraine 216

High Cross 211

South Tottenham 321

Park 105

Bruce Grove 373

Tottenham Central 375

Seven Sisters 207

White Hart Lane 101

West Green 442

Green Lanes 397

Woodside 401

Noel Park 405

Harringay 590

South Hornsey 271

Hornsey Vale 238

Bowes Park 413

Hornsey Central 236

Crouch End 293

Alexandra 251

Muswell Hill 260

Archway 113

Fortis Green 210

Highgate 121

Source – 1981 Census Small Area Statistics (100%) Ward Data

N.B. Total for each ward shown on map

79

Appendix 2: 1981 Census

1981 Census
Small Area Statistics

Place of Birth – Asian Population in L.B. of Haringey

	East Africa			India			Bangladesh			Pakistan			Total Asian Pop	Total Pop	Asian as % Total
	M	F	Total	M	F	Total	M	F	Total	M	F	Total			
Alexandra	62	42	104	73	76	149	3	3	6	6	2	8	267	9500	2.8
Archway	31	19	50	26	31	57	–	–	–	5	5	10	117	6186	1.9
Bowes Park	150	108	258	129	131	260	10	8	18	21	18	39	575	11183	5.1
Bruce Grove	90	60	150	106	101	207	15	14	29	39	31	70	456	11250	4.1
Coleraine	42	32	74	76	74	150	10	2	12	10	5	15	251	10545	2.4
Crouch End	33	43	76	73	72	145	19	13	32	14	7	21	274	8281	3.3
Fortis Green	31	34	65	63	65	128	13	6	19	8	8	16	228	9177	2.5
Green Lanes	56	53	109	80	71	151	26	22	48	44	29	73	381	8054	4.7
Harringay	154	142	296	123	115	238	59	51	110	42	35	77	721	11037	6.5
High Cross	47	40	87	60	63	123	18	19	37	10	9	19	266	7049	3.8
Highgate	33	27	60	26	24	50	7	5	12	6	4	10	132	6378	2.1
Hornsey Central	63	59	122	80	82	162	16	12	28	8	–	8	320	6662	4.8
Hornsey Vale	53	48	101	77	58	135	13	9	22	12	14	26	284	6358	4.5
Muswell Hill	24	27	51	66	67	133	6	6	12	9	6	15	211	10331	2.0
Noel Park	101	104	205	112	122	234	36	29	65	7	15	22	526	10706	4.9
Park	24	34	58	35	31	66	4	1	5	4	6	10	139	6765	2.1
Seven Sisters	37	33	70	45	38	83	13	10	23	20	16	36	212	6772	3.1
South Hornsey	41	34	75	74	54	128	21	16	37	14	12	26	266	6484	4.1
South Tottenham	28	27	55	101	97	198	11	10	21	21	18	39	313	7607	4.1
Tottenham Central	64	65	129	117	109	226	25	15	40	30	24	54	449	10920	4.1
West Green	94	86	180	104	101	205	40	35	75	19	16	35	495	11665	4.2
White Hart Lane	25	23	48	32	35	67	1	–	1	9	8	17	133	10011	1.3
Woodside	130	100	230	123	146	269	24	15	39	10	11	21	559	9720	5.7
Total	1413	1240	2653	1801	1763	3564	390	301	691	368	299	667	7575	202641	3.7

Appendix 3: Letter sent out to the sample in English and Asian languages introducing the project

PROJECT SUPPORTED BY HARINGEY SOCIAL SERVICES

DATE AS POSTMARK

Dear

BETTER HEALTH SERVICES FOR ASIANS

A project has been set up to research and develop health services for Asians in the borough of Haringey.

Our project aims to bring into focus the importance of recognising the health needs of the Asian community so that:

a) professionals are trained to respect and respond positively to our community's perceptions.

b) service delivery makes provision for cultural and religious needs on a routine basis.

It is important that your views and experiences are considered to enable a clearer understanding of the issues.

We would therefore request a brief interview with you at a time that is convenient.

We will be contacting you in the near future. We look forward to your co-operation in this matter.

Thanking you,

Yours sincerely

হ্যারিংগে সোশাল সার্ভিসের দ্বারা সমর্থিত প্রজেক্ট

এশিয়ানদের জন্য আরও ভাল হেলথ সার্ভিস

হ্যারিংগে বারোতে এশিয়ানদের জন্য হেলথ সার্ভিসের সরবরন ও উন্নতসাধন করতে একটি কর্মপরিকল্পনা প্রতিষ্ঠা করা হয়েছে।

এশিয়ান কমিউনিটির স্বাস্থ্যের প্রয়োজনীয়তার স্বীকৃতি দেওয়ার গুরুত্বর আলোকপাত করা আমাদের প্রজেক্টের উদ্দেশ্য যার দ্বারা এগুলি সম্ভব হবে : যেমন,

ক) পেশাদারীরা আমাদের কমিউনিটির অনুভূতিকে সঠিকভাবে সম্মান দিতে এবং সাড়া দিতে শেখেন।

খ) নিয়মিতভাবে সাংস্কৃতিক ও ধর্মীয় প্রয়োজনের বিধি জন্য সার্ভিস প্রদান করা যাবে।

এই বিষয় সুলি পারিস্কার করে বুঝতে সক্ষম হওয়ার জন্য আপনার মতামত এবং অভিজ্ঞতা বিবেচনা করা খুব গুরুত্বপূর্ন।

সেজন্য আপনার সুবিধামত এমন এক সময়ে আপনার সাথে সংক্ষিপ্ত সাক্ষাৎকারের জন্য অনুরোধ করছি।

খুব শীঘ্রই আমরা আপনার সাথে যোগাযোগ করব। এই বিষয়ে আমরা আপনার সহযোগিতা পাওয়ার আশায় রয়েছি।

ধন্যবাদ-

আপনার বিনীত

ડૅરીંગે સોશ્યલ સર્વીસીઝના સહકારથી ચાલતી યોજના

પોસ્ટના સિક્કા પર જે તારીખ હોય તે

એશિયનો માટે વધુ સારી આરોગ્ય સેવાઓ

ડૅરીંગે બરોમાં વસી રહેલા એશિયનોને મળતી આરોગ્ય સેવાઓનું સંશોધન કરી તેને વિકસાવવા માટે આ યોજના સ્થાપવામાં આવી છે.

અમારી યોજનાનો આશય છે કે એશિયન કૉમ્યુનિટિની આરોગ્ય ક્ષેત્રમાં જે જરૂરિયાતો છે તેને ઓળખવાની આવશ્યકતાને કૅન્દ્રિત કરવી, જેથી :

અ. અમારી કૉમ્યુનિટિ વિશેના અવલોકનને જ્ઞાન આપે અને તેના તરફ નિશ્ચયાત્મક વલણ ધરાવે તેવી કેળવણી અમે અમારા નિષ્ણાતોને આપી શકીએ.

બ. જે સેવા અમે આપીએ તેમાં સાંસ્કૃતિક અને ધાર્મિક જરૂરિયાતોને રોજંદી પ્રથા ગણી પૂરી પાડવામાં આવે.

આ વિષયના જુદા જુદા મુદ્દાઓને સચોટ રીતે સમજી શકવામાં અમને મદદ મળે તે માટે તમારા મંતવ્યો અને અનુભવો મેળવવા જરૂરી છે.

તેથી અમે ઈચ્છીએ છીએ કે તમને યોગ્ય હોય તે સમયે અમે તમારી ટૂંકી મુલાકાત લઈએ.

નજીકમાં અમે તમારો સંપર્ક સાધીશું. આ બાબતમાં તમારો સહકાર અમને મળશે તેવી આશા રાખીએ છીએ.

આભાર સહિત,
તમારા શુભેચ્છક

GUJARATI

83

हैरिंगे समाज सेवा द्वारा समर्थित योजना

रशियन लोगों के लिये अच्छी स्वास्थ्य सेवाएं

हैरिंगे बरो में रशियन लोगों के लिये, स्वास्थ्य सेवा में विकास और अनुसन्धान हेतु एक योजना स्थापित की गई है।

रशियन समाज की स्वास्थ्य सम्बन्धी जरूरतों की मान्यता के महत्व को केन्द्रित करना ही हमारी योजना का उद्देश्य है ताकि :

अ) हमारे समाज की अनुभूतियों को सकारात्मक अनुक्रिया और सम्मान हेतु वृत्तिकों के प्रशिक्षण दिया जाये।

ब) सेवा वितरण में, सामान्य आधार पर धार्मिक और सांस्कृतिक जरूरतों के लिये प्रबन्ध हो।

यह आवश्यक है कि विषयों को स्पष्ट रूप से समझने के लिये आप के विचारों और अनुभवों पर ध्यान दिये जायें।

इस लिये, आप की सुविधा के समय पर, आप से एक संक्षिप्त भेंट (इन्टरव्यु) का निवेदन करेंगे।

निकट भविष्य में हम आप से सम्पर्क करेंगे। इस विषय में, हम आप के सहयोग की आशा रखते हैं।

आप का धन्यवाद

भवदीय

HINDI

84

ਇਸ ਪ੍ਰੋਜੈਕਟ ਨੂੰ 'ਹੈਰਿੰਗੇ ਸੋਸ਼ਲ ਸਰਵਿਸਿਜ਼' ਵਲੋਂ ਸਮਰਥਨ ਹੈ ।

ਤਰੀਕ ਡਾਕ- ਮੋਹਰ ਵਾਲੀ

ਏਸ਼ਿਅਨ ਲੋਕਾਂ ਲਈ ਚੰਗੀਆਂ ਸਿਹਤ ਸੇਵਾਂ

'ਬਾਰੋ ਆਫ ਹੈਰਿੰਗੇ' ਨੇ ਏਸ਼ਿਅਨ ਲੋਕਾਂ ਦੀਆਂ ਸਿਹਤ ਸੇਵਾਂ ਬਾਰੇ ਖੋਜ ਕਰਨ ਅਤੇ ਵਾਧਾ ਦੇਣ ਲਈ ਇਹ ਪ੍ਰੋਜੈਕਟ ਆਰੰਭਿਆ ਹੈ ।

ਸਾਡੇ ਪ੍ਰੋਜੈਕਟ ਦਾ ਮੰਤਵ ਏਸ਼ਿਅਨ ਕਮਿਊਨਿਟੀ ਦੀਆਂ ਸਿਹਤ ਬਾਰੇ ਲੋੜਾਂ ਦੀ ਮਹੱਤਤਾ ਤੋਂ ਜਾਣੂ ਕਰਵਾਉਣਾ ਹੈ ਤਾਂ ਜੋ :

(ੲ) ਏਸ਼ਿਅਨ ਕਮਿਊਨਿਟੀ ਦੇ ਪ੍ਰਤੱਖ ਗਿਆਨ ਨੂੰ ਸਹੀ ਤੌਰ ਤੇ ਜਾਨਣ ਲਈ ਪੇਸ਼ਾਵਰਾਂ ਨੂੰ ਟ੍ਰੇਨਿੰਗ ਦਿੱਤੀ ਜਾ ਸਕੇ ।

(ਅ) ਏਸ਼ਿਅਨ ਕਮਿਊਨਿਟੀ ਦੀ ਸਭਿਅਤਾ ਅਤੇ ਧਾਰਮਕ ਲੋੜਾਂ ਦੇ ਰੋਜ਼ਾਨਾ ਅਧਾਰ ਅਨੁਸਾਰ ਸੇਵਾ ਕਰਨ ਲਈ ਪ੍ਰਬੰਧ ਕੀਤਾ ਜਾ ਸਕੇ।

ਇਹ ਬੜਾ ਹੀ ਮਹੱਤਵਪੂਰਣ ਹੈ ਕਿ ਮਸਲਿਆਂ ਨੂੰ ਚੰਗੀ ਤਰਾਂ ਸਮਝਣ ਲਈ ਤੁਹਾਡੇ ਉਦੇਸ਼ਾਂ ਤੇ ਤਜਰਬਿਆਂ ਨੂੰ ਵਿਚਾਰਿਆ ਜਾਵੇ।

ਇਸ ਕਰਕੇ ਕਿਸੇ ਠੀਕ ਸਮੇਂ ਤੇ ਆਪ ਨਾਲ ਰੱਲ ਬਾਤ ਕਰਨ ਲਈ ਬੇਨਤੀ ਕੀਤੀ ਜਾਂਦੀ ਹੈ ।

ਅਸੀਂ ਭੋਤੀ ਹੀ ਆਉਣ ਵਾਲੇ ਸਮੇਂ ਵਿੱਚ ਤੁਹਾਨੂੰ ਪਹੁੰਚ ਕਰਾਂਗੇ। ਇਸ ਮਾਮਲੇ ਵਿੱਚ ਆਪਦੇ ਮਿਲਵਰਤਣ ਲਈ ਆਸ਼ਾਵਾਦੀ ਹਾਂ ।

ਧੰਨਵਾਦ ਸਹਿਤ।

ਆਪਦਾ ਸ਼ੁਭ- ਇੱਛਕ,

اس پراجیکٹ کو ہیرنگے سوشل سروسیز کی طرف سے امداد ملتی ہے

اس خط کی تاریخ لفافے کی مہر کے مطابق ہے

ایشیائی لوگوں کی صحت کے لئے بہتر ہیلتھ سروسیں

ہیرنگے بوراؤ میں رہنے والے ایشیائی لوگوں کی صحت کے لئے ہیلتھ سروسوں میں تحقیقات کرنے اور انکو تشکیل دینے کے لئے ایک پراجیکٹ قائم کیا گیا ہے ۔

ہمارے پراجیکٹ کا مقصد ایشیائی لوگوں کی صحت کی ضروریات کو تسلیم کرنے کی اہمیت پر توجہ دلانا ہے تاکہ :

الف) ہمارے ایشیائی لوگوں کے احساسات کا لحاظ رکھنے اور واقعی طور پر انکے احساسات کے مطابق کام کرنے کے لئے پیشہ ور لوگوں کو ٹریننگ دی جا سکے ۔

ب) بطور حسب معمول ایشیائی لوگوں کو سروس بہم پہنچانے میں انکی سماجی اور مذہبی ضروریات کا خیال رکھا جا سکے ۔

ایشیائی لوگوں کے مسائل کو اچھی طرح سمجھنے کے لئے یہ ضروری ہے کہ آپ کے نظریات اور تجربات کو سمجھا جائے ۔

اس مقصد کے لئے ہم آپ سے موزوں وقت میں ایک مختصر سی ملاقات (انٹرویو) کرنا چاہتے ہیں ۔

ہم عنقریب آپ سے رابطہ قائم کرینگے ۔ اس معاملہ میں ہمیں آپ کے تعاون کی امید ہے ۔

شکریہ
مخلص

Appendix 4: First recall letter

Dear

I wrote to you recently asking whether you are willing to take part in a project concerned with Better Health Services for Asians.

I hope you will not object to me visiting you in your home in connection with this study.

Since we could not contact you over the phone to arrange a time, I would like to suggest the following date and time for the visit:

_____ at _____.

I do hope you will be available at this time. It is so important to have your views so that services can be treated as confidential.

If this time is inconvenient or if you have any objection to this visit please let me know as soon as possible.

Yours sincerely

Appendix 5: Second recall letter

Dear

As arranged, I called on you at _____today.

Unfortunately you were not in at that time. I would still like
to meet you as your views are very important. I would like to
suggest the following date and time for the next visit:

_____ at _____.

I do hope to see you then. However if this is not a suitable
time for you, please let me know as soon as possible.

Yours sincerely